Josie Arlington's Storyville

Josie Arlington's Storyville

THE LIFE AND TIMES OF A NEW ORLEANS MADAM

MARITA WOYWOD CRANDLE

THE
History
PRESS

Published by The History Press
Charleston, SC
www.historypress.com

First published 2020

Manufactured in the United States

ISBN 9781467142540

Library of Congress Control Number: 2019951988

*This book is dedicated to Darlene Brocato,
her family and the many ancestors of
the woman who called herself Josie Arlington
for allowing us to celebrate the legacy she left
to the city of New Orleans.*

CONTENTS

FOREWORD

New Orleans has a way of bringing magic into people's lives. It was a complete coincidence that Marita mentioned to me she was writing a book about Josie Arlington. I had known Marita for about seventeen years casually as a customer, first at Tujague's on Decatur and now Vincent's on St. Charles. One day out of the blue, she told me she was going to write her next book about Josie Arlington. I remember asking her why before I told her Josie was my ancestor. I also remember the look on Marita's face. It was like I had just told her Santa Claus was real. It has been a fun project working with Marita on this book.

My mother, Marie Deubler Tanet, would tell me stories of my grandfather's aunt "Josie" when we were growing up. "*Fidusa*," she would say, meaning "filthy one," when I didn't want to get in the bath. "You're a dirty little girl. Do you want to be a *butona* [tramp] like Josie?" I used to laugh. It wasn't until my mother and her cousin started doing our family genealogy that I became so interested in the life of Josie Arlington.

We had a vase in our house that was salvaged from the Arlington brothel, and later my mother inherited it from her cousin. I always thought it was the tackiest, ugliest vase, but now I love it. The things that vase has seen!

My mother also inherited a few dining utensils that Josie had commissioned someone to make for herself and her brothers, Henry and Peter Deubler. When, we don't know, but she was already going by the name Josie at the time. She was of course born Mary Deubler, but she liked the name Josie. I now cherish the few items I have inherited from my mother: the vase, Josie's napkin ring, her brother Henry's spoon and her other brother Peter's fork.

Darlene Brocato, ancestor of Josie Arlington, in front of the tomb Josie had built for herself in 1911. *Author's collection.*

Top: A vase salvaged from the Arlington brothel and passed down to Josie's family. It is now in the possession of Darlene Brocato. *Author's collection*.

Middle: A sterling silver napkin ring created for Josie Deubler sometime in the late 1800s. It is now in the possession of Darlene Brocato. *Author's collection*.

Bottom: The napkin ring and a fork and spoon created for Henry and Peter Deubler sometime in the late 1800s. They are now in the possession of Darlene Brocato. *Author's collection*.

Josie was such an important part of New Orleans history. Not only did she own the most palatial brothel in Storyville, but I remember all the stories my mother would tell me about the land she donated to the churches here and across the river. She really became an important philanthropist for New Orleans. She also provided for her family for much of her young life after she became a prostitute and ultimately until the end of her life.

Josie Arlington (Mary Deubler) was a romantic and wanted desperately to be in love. It is so ironic that she died on February 14, 1914, Valentine's Day. While I believe she enjoyed her life, New Orleans style, she also was somewhat of a tortured soul.

People ask me all the time about her, and it seems a little odd to be so proud to be related to someone who made her fame and fortune as a madam. However, it is such an important part of New Orleans culture and one of the oldest professions in the world. Storyville was a neighborhood like no other. I'm proud to be her descendant. She was a strong woman, and my mother was the same. I have certainly inherited her spirit.

When I think of Josie Arlington, I think about the times when some madams lit voodoo ritual candles for money and love. I think of Storyville and the music and flavor that has led to who we are today. I think of a strong girl who made a path for herself, her way and how her genes run through me.

Josie Arlington was New Orleans.

—Darlene Tanet Brocato

ACKNOWLEDGEMENTS

Thank you to Darlene Brocato for sharing her family stories and recollections. Without her, this book would not be whole. Thank you to Robert Ticknor of the Historic New Orleans Collection for his always enthusiastic willingness to help and his outstanding knowledge of New Orleans history. Thank you to my editor, Joe Gartrell, for his hard work and enthusiasm with this project. Thank you to my assistant, Anne Guthrie, for her enthusiasm, endless reading and editing and creative ideas. Thank you to my husband, Steven Crandle, for taking care of everything else on all those days I spent doing research and writing, locked in our home office. Thank you to my Boutique du Vampyre and Potions staff—Lia, Kim, Tory, Kia, April, Alys, Erika, Kate, Rachel, Jake, Steven, Mike, Rhonda and Yvaine—for picking up the slack and allowing me to work worry free. Thank you to the city of New Orleans for inspiring our magnificent culture.

INTRODUCTION

Gray is the color that sometimes best describes the city of New Orleans, not because of its often hazy damp days or moist foggy mornings but because of the gray area that defines the city's culture. From a sordid, gritty, hopeful and colorful past, the city has become known for its nonjudgmental people with their accepting attitude and a love for life. *Laissez les bons temps rouler*!—the Cajun French expression for "Let the good times roll!"—is often heard in New Orleans and used in artwork throughout the city.

Perhaps that can help one understand why someone like Josie Arlington, who also stemmed from a questionable beginning and lived a precarious life, might be celebrated as a New Orleans icon. Nothing about Josie was black or white. Forced out on her own at a young age, having owned the most dangerous brothel in the city to then the most palatial, she was a fighter, a lover, a pioneer, a caretaker and a philanthropist. Her story takes us through New Orleans's Storyville history with its industrious and crafty politicians, its musical roots and its legalized prostitution.

Her life was shaped by circumstances and strong will that found her first a prostitute as a young woman and not much later a madam. She lived at a time when Storyville put its mark on the city, clearing the path for profitable women-owned businesses. It's said she prided herself on the moral that no virgin would be deflowered at her establishment. She was an entrepreneur who was creative, hardworking and sometimes colorfully deceitful.

St. Louis Cathedral in the fog, French Quarter, New Orleans. *Courtesy Mark Barrett.*

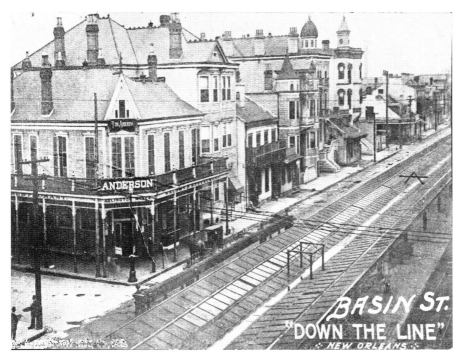

The brothels of Basin Street, circa 1900. Photo by E.J. Bellocq. *Hogan Jazz Archive Photography Collection, Tulane University Special Collections, Howard-Tilton Memorial Library, Tulane University.*

Josie and the other scarlet women of the "Tenderloin" went places and saw things the respectable women of the city despised—and some may have secretly envied, including long nights with dancing, drinking, politics, brawls and even murder. It was an exciting time and surely not for the genteel.

While Josie's choice of profession may have been questionable, she was able to employ many family members in various aspects of her businesses and her estate. It's an interesting fact that her family came from a long line of seamstresses. Josie's cousin Margaret McLaffen was employed by Josie and other madams in the neighborhood. McLaffen passed her talents down to her ancestors, as her current descendants also are well-known seamstresses in the city, creating elaborate Mardi Gras gowns and costumes to this day.

Other family members tended to her properties, even taking care of livestock at her farm in Abita Springs. She created an enterprise of sorts with the opportunities made available to her. Over the years, she transformed herself from a scrappy prostitute to a woman of means who traveled with her lover and lived in her own exquisite mansion on a lovely New Orleans tree-lined street in a fine neighborhood.

Her life ended as unusually as it began with a strange and questionable love affair, a contested will, an elaborate tomb and a ghost story. Characters like Josie Arlington and their fascinating legacies forever leave their mark on our city and the culture that New Orleans has become so famous for.

Finding adequate documentation to follow the life of one particular character through New Orleans history in a linear fashion was a challenge. Without repeating much of what has already been written, I have done my best to piece together only facts to explain who Josie Arlington was. I am very grateful to our wonderful libraries and city and university archives that had the foresight to maintain documents including contracts, family photographs and architectural plans to help us understand the life and times of Josie Arlington.

Chapter I

THE ENVIRONMENT FOR PROSTITUTION IN NEW ORLEANS

From day one, New Orleans has worn the mark of the scarlet letter, first due to the very poor direction of John Law and his Company of the Indies. Law, a Scotsman, was hired by the king of France with questionable attempts to colonize New Orleans. His very aggressive and thoughtless means of populating the city had criminals and prostitutes brought from France to Louisiana against their will. It's not surprising that prostitution dug its heels in the city, with such a history of illicitness from its very birth. For the entire early eighteenth century, a priority in the colonization of New Orleans was devising plans to attract women to the city to help hold the attention of the men who would, in turn, create families to colonize the territory. These families would work the land, develop housing and engage in traditional businesses, trade and activities found in any functioning community.

However, a "normal" community was far from how New Orleans could have been characterized. With the development of the port city, and the cast of characters who helped build it, came sketchy attributes. At the time of the Civil War, vice districts had organized in every major United States city, as well as many sparsely populated territories in the Deep South to trade liquor for prostitution and gambling. But there was none like that which had materialized in New Orleans. With downtown New Orleans emerged two all-but-forgotten vice districts that became the wretched forefathers of Storyville and were known at the time as the Vieux Carre and the Swamp. The Vieux Carre sat behind the upper French Quarter where Basin Street met Customhouse (now called Iberville) and Customhouse ran to Franklin and the back end of the area faded into the swampy terrain. The district known as the Swamp festered on the land that is now the Central Business District, the Warehouse District and the Lower Garden District.

In his book *Storyville, New Orleans*, Al Rose describes the territory as "an incredible jumble of cheap dancehalls, brothels, saloons and gaming rooms, cockfighting pits and rooming houses. A one-story shantytown jammed into a half-dozen teeming blocks, the Swamp was the scene of some eight hundred known murders between 1820 and 1850."

Police avoided the neighborhood, or rather, they allowed those who entered the Swamp to handle their own affairs. "A man could wander into the Swamp and for the going rate of a picayune [about six cents] obtain a bed for the night, a drink of whiskey, and a woman." It seems that the men it attracted were the kind who carried little more than six cents, or it would not have lasted long. The lowest of the low passed through the Swamp to spend what little they had on the even more desperate, deteriorated and pitiful who had found themselves stuck in the hell called the Swamp. The Swamp lost some momentum in the late 1850s with a shift of business heading to the other side of the French Quarter.

The very busy port at the end of Esplanade Street created yet another outlet for those who set foot in the city. Gallatin Street, two blocks in totality, became so foul that entire buildings were eventually demolished to erase the stigma of the character of men and women they once housed. Richard Campanella writes in his book *Bourbon Street: A History* that the short two blocks between Ursulines and Barracks became known as the "thoroughfare." The seedy section was avoided by any respectable citizen but sought out by those looking for a raunchy and rowdy rendezvous. Campanella references newspaper articles at the time characterizing the women who worked the street with reputations that had those in the city acknowledging them as "the frail daughters of Gallatin Street." If you mentioned that a woman had a career on Gallatin Street, it was immediately understood what that profession was. The women were pitied and demoralized in general conversation.

Like a moat of solicitous debauchery, the neighborhoods flaunting liquor, gambling and loose women framed the city of New Orleans. Gallatin Street was close to the prime market area with thriving, steady twenty-four-hour traffic that attracted criminals and prostitutes who took advantage of those with fat pockets and the quick jobs and cheap meals found in the neighborhood.

Historian and professor of history at Tulane University Judith Schafer, in her book *Brothels, Depravity, and Abandoned Women: Illegal Sex in Antebellum*

New Orleans, explains that in 1857, the city council passed a sixteen-act piece of legislation known as the Lorette Law, named for what the French call prostitutes. The ordinance helped to push prostitution from the river back to the fringe of the city at Customhouse and Basin, where the law was not in effect. The ordinance was specific to a dedicated geography in which prostitutes would annually be taxed $100 and the head of the house $250. While prostitution was still legal on the second floors of buildings on Gallatin, it was not legal for women to work from the ground floor or stand in their doorways or on the streets in front of their houses. "The spatial restrictions aimed to make the sex trade invisible." Furthermore, prostitutes were not allowed to coax customers from cafés or coffeehouses.

Rather than pay the tax, the flux of business moved to Customhouse and Basin, where the law was not in effect. Before the Lorette Law, there had been very loose laws regarding prostitution. Primarily, the orders were directed at keeping neighborhoods peaceful and did not focus on the issue of sex for hire. However, the law was immediately attacked by all involved in the business of prostitution, and on a technicality of licensing, it was ruled unconstitutional in 1859, upon which, in New Orleans tradition, a parade was thrown to celebrate. However, this one, profane and in poor spirit, gave the finger to the city as it marched through the streets.

In a new renovation program many years later, the city chose to demolish the then underused buildings that lined Gallatin Street. The area had great potential, but after the brothels had fled the area, the street attracted nothing but vagrants. In 1935, the city demolished all the buildings and gave the area a fresh start. Gallatin was renamed French Market Place and not long after turned into a farmers' market.

However, the next phase of wickedness was finding its place along the vice district that had been known as the Vieux Carre. Basin Street—whose name comes from the turning basin of the Carondelet Canal, which had been located on the street in the section where it now turns on to Orleans—would soon be known as the iconic "Down the Line," the row of Storyville brothel palaces. At that time, the brothels were much less than palaces run by madams such as Minnie Ha Ha, Kate Townsend and Hattie Hamilton.

It was only a couple of decades later that a young Josie Arlington found her way to Customhouse Street. The environment was a bit more "civilized" by the time her story began. Yet her time in the profession before Storyville could still be considered rough and dangerous—perhaps just not as barbaric as the era of the Swamp and Gallatin Street.

Chapter 2

MARY DEUBLER

THE EARLY YEARS

The late 1800s in New Orleans was an exciting time for those in the city. New Orleans had been the most profitable city in America and the third largest. While census information documents the growth of the city slowing toward the latter half of the nineteenth century, the city was still advancing in a variety of ways.

New Orleans had fought its way through a volatile history under John Law, who, in addition to shipping the derelicts to the city, encouraged others to come from Germany and Italy at his invitation, with great anticipation of reaping the fortunes they had been misled to believe were available to them. These immigrants instead found swamps with land that was difficult or impossible to farm. Yet the depressed economic climate in Germany had people looking for alternate homesteads, and tens of thousands of Germans immigrated to New Orleans. The 1840s and early 1850s peaked with German immigrants flooding into the port of New Orleans, joining their family and friends with hopes of making better lives for themselves.

Germans, in fact, have been credited through their hard work in farming land as having greatly contributed to the settlement of New Orleans. A city not far from New Orleans, known as Des Allemands (which means "the Germans" in French), was once owned by John Law. He sold it off to German settlers, a little at a time, making a nice profit for himself. In 1857, the German Society of New Orleans was established in order to help German immigrants become acclimated in the new country.

There has been much speculation over Josie Arlington's past during her younger years in the city of New Orleans. Born Mary Anna Deubler, she and her two brothers, Henry and Peter, were raised in New Orleans by strict German immigrant parents. A story handed down by her family is that Mary had a definite curfew that was not to be broken. Yet one night at the age of seventeen, she missed that curfew, and in extreme anger, her parents put their foot down and would not let her return to their home. This is also the version told in the book *Queen New Orleans* (1949), by Harnett T. Kane:

> *A certain Lobrano took her to dinner and did not bring her home until nearly eleven o'clock. This, of course, could mean only one thing. Her father slammed the door, and, though Josie knocked and knocked, he kept it barred against her. Meanwhile Lobrano was waiting outside. He was afraid he couldn't support her; but he had another suggestion: She would support him. He knew one or two madams; with his backing, she could do well for herself.*

However, Josie told a very different story to her niece Anna Deubler. She claimed that she was orphaned at a young age and forced to live with her mother's sister, who treated her unfairly. Josie told the same version during a court case later in her life, explaining why she briefly went by the name Schultz, which she says was her aunt's name. As reported in the *Times-Picayune* of January 29, 1892, during the trial of her brother's murder, "My right name is Mary A. Deubler. Was raised by an aunt named Schultz and was once known by that name."

No one knows to what extent each version is reliable, but these were serious times for Josie and her family, and one way or another, the situation catapulted a young Mary Deubler into a life of prostitution.

Over the years, as mentioned, she went by various aliases, including Mary Nix, Josie Deubler, Josie Schultz, Josie Alton and Josie Lobrano, most likely to protect her family while she worked at various brothels on Customhouse and Basin Streets. The thriving port brought business to the city and, with it, a flurry of sailors who found New Orleans catering to their desire to let loose while at port. Drinking, gaming and women were among the top priorities, allowing prostitution to thrive.

In 1885, Josie is listed in a city directory for prostitution as the head of a home, under the name Miss Josie Lobrano, the surname of her then lover, Philip Lobrano, yet the two were never married. Josie had a strong will and an entrepreneurial nature, and at the time, prostitution was one of the few businesses women had the right to manage. From prostitute to madam,

Josie Arlington sometime in the late 1800s. *From the Josie Arlington Collection, courtesy Earl K. Long Library, University of New Orleans.*

Josie soon ran a brothel on the corner of Burgundy and Customhouse, on the seedier side of the city. The brothels were close to the city's opium dens and all under the ominous watch of the enormous prison known as the Metropolis.

The opium dens were hidden in the Chinese laundromats that lined Rampart Street and other areas of the city. A local rag, or independent journal, the *Mascot*, published in New Orleans on Saturdays from 1882 to 1897, referenced the cover cartoon in its August 3, 1889 edition:

> *It would surprise many persons if they only knew to what a frightful extent the opium habit has taken hold in New Orleans. It may not be generally known but a matter of fact, more people in New Orleans are addicted to the enslaving and totally demoralizing habit than in any other city of the union. The opium "joints" flourish in all parts of the city and are patronized by*

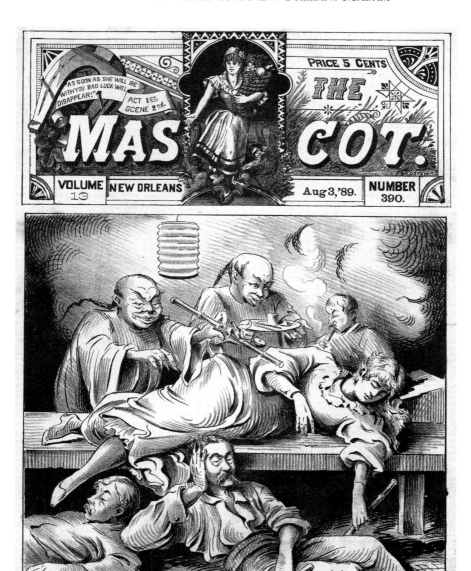

Cover of the *Mascot*, August 3, 1989. *Courtesy Tulane University Special Collections, Howard-Tilton Memorial Library, Tulane University.*

all classes. There locations are known not only by the regular "fiends" but also to many other people besides the police, who are not regular customers. Almost every Chinese laundry in New Orleans is an opium joint, where the lovers of the "pipe" can be accommodated and the wonder is that some determined and positive effort has not already been made to suppress the frightful evil to which so many of our people are enslaved. The Chinese joints are not frequented exclusively by the women of the town as may be generally expected but are liberally patronized by young women and old ones too, who are respectable and move in others than out-cast circles.

It was easy to find what you wanted in the city of New Orleans in all forms of vices. Not even the vast metropolis of a building that was erected in the 1880s, where the New Orleans public library stands today, could threaten those driven to find decadence. The building served as the city's criminal court and parish prison. Towering over the debauchery below, it housed three hundred prison cells for men and fifty for women, offices for the judges, the courthouse, a chapel and a yard where hangings were performed.

The city that was born under the corruption of John Law continued the tradition. When the Orleans Parish Criminal Court building was erected in the 1880s, it quickly began to crack and creak. Floors shifted and walls splintered. At first, those in charge chalked it up to the soft soil of New Orleans and the high water table. However, not long after it was discovered that the very individuals in charge of building the structure had cunningly cut corners and, in good old New Orleans fashion, filled their pockets instead of putting the money where it belonged. They were all arrested, and poetic justice had them placed in the prison they had built. Nicknamed "The Metropolis" for its ominous Gothic beauty, the building sadly lasted only forty years.

The climate in New Orleans for indulgence was so great that justification for vices became greater than the threat of tainting the good people of the city. Even the law found it hard to keep hands out of the cookie jar. A few police officers found their way to corruption among the corrupt. In fact, a court case was filed against two officers, Patrick J. Bell and John P. Bayhi, in 1893 for blackmailing prostitutes. They were offering their "protection" for weekly payment, reportedly around two dollars per prostitute. The scandal shook up the police force with allegations of not just those officers but against the entire force, including "greatly incompetent men among its commanding officers."

Feeling vindicated in the acknowledgement of a crime against them, the prostitutes of the city showed up in full force. An article published on

Old Orleans Parish Criminal Court and Old Parish Prison. *Courtesy Southeastern Architectural Archive, Special Collections Division, Tulane University Libraries.*

September 1, 1893, paints a wonderful picture of the scene, with everyone gathering for a day in court:

> *The room filled with a motley assembly. The corridors in the immediate vicinity of the Council Chamber were thronged. Men and women were there, the men mostly as spectators, the women all as witnesses.*
>
> *Outside the hall the scene presented almost resembled that outside the French Opera House of a winter's night. Lamps flashed in long rows up and down the street. Stamping horses attached to carriages and cabs waited for hours for the women inside the building.*
>
> *In the council chamber itself the scene while scarcely to be dignified by the term brilliant, was a gaudy one in the extreme.*

It was described as an event so extraordinary that one like it would hardly grace the courthouse again. One can only imagine the cast of mixed-up characters coming to say their piece, parading through the courthouse halls in impossible costumes:

There were women dressed in all the colors of the rainbow. They were dressed in rustling silks and satins, they were dressed in rags. Costly diamonds flashed and glittered from ears and arms, from bosoms and from fingers; disease and dirt showed itself plainly on countenance and figure, on dress and manure.

Women old and women young, women white and women black, painted or haggard, successful and starving, they made up the most representative group of beings belonging to the world's necessary social evil, yelept [sic] from time immemorial "scarlet women."

A cornucopia of amusing-looking women standing up for their rights, indignant and justified, were in full force, from the "palaces of vice on Customhouse street" to the "hovels and thieving dens of Burgundy street." If they weren't already making a statement, the most notorious of them took it one step further, enjoying the assembly as great entertainment. The subhead read "They Drank Champagne":

The queens of the demi-mode Annie Decker, Josie Lobrano Arlington and Press Meyers made the occasion of their first appearance in the Council Chamber a festive one. They acted in the public hall as if they were at home. Feeling dry they called one of their coachmen and sent him off for some bottles of champagne. They sat in the front row of chairs behind the spectator's rail.

Apparently, they offered champagne to the gentlemen seated around them, but all declined, and those in charge at the courthouse must not have seen the libations, or else the ladies might have been interrupted.

The courageous women faced parole officers one at a time during an era when corruption in the force was at an all-time high. Preying on prostitutes who could scarcely pay for the tattered clothes they sported and the shabby rooms they rented showed the character of the officers the prostitutes were up against. But even those women with the scarcest of means were made to feel proud among their somewhat more "sophisticated" contemporaries on this day.

Reportedly, most of the women were of the lesser status and appeared to be around fifty years of age, and certainly few younger than thirty. They were told to speak the truth and not hold back as to how the police had abused their position of power against the prostitutes. While they were not represented by counsel, they were guaranteed protection by the board, and all in attendance listened eagerly as, one by one, the circus of women testified.

Officers Bell and Bayhi were immediately released from the force. There were higher men implicated during the course of the case, from the chief on down. The case shook up the department and instilled confidence in the women of ill repute. It gave the women just the boost they needed to forge ahead, turning the oldest profession into a recognized legal one.

Chapter 3

DIAMONDS IN HER HAIR

Josie seemed to have fallen into a less than luxurious life; however, her drive for success had her quickly running a brothel of her own. Located at 172 Customhouse Street (now Iberville) and Burgundy, Josie quickly took the reins and ran other prostitutes, making enough money to care for her family.

The brothel on Customhouse she ran with her boyfriend, Philip Lobrano, an Italian. It was thought to be one of the grittiest houses of prostitution in the city. The place was rowdy and attracted the gruffest of clientele, with fights breaking out almost nightly between prostitutes as well as with their clients.

Josie held a nasty reputation as a fighter as well. At the time, it was a practice to keep items of value in the hairstyle worn at the time, known as a pompadour. Josie's descendant Darlene Brocato recollects a story handed down that her great-aunt often hid diamonds in her hair. A newspaper at the time reported that in a fight with a prostitute, Beulah Ripley, the altercation was so violent that Ripley left the scene missing part of her ear and lip and Josie a large portion of her hair. One wonders if Ripley found the diamonds.

Beulah Ripley seemed to stay in trouble as well. A prostitute at Mrs. Haley's house, located at 180 Customhouse Street, she was arrested several times. On one such instance, while seated in front of the affidavit clerk, both Ripley and her counterpart became so unruly that the judge ordered their arrests immediately. However, with a little time to cool off, they were once again heard, and the judge let them off with "an iron-clad reprimand and warning, permitted them to depart and sin no more."

It was a dangerous time for young women wanting to escape a desperate life. In his book *Storyville New Orleans*, Al Rose writes of the young virgins who were slaves, runaways, escaping from some other peril or abducted and their virginity sold at a premium. Apparently, Mary Thompson used her cigar shop on Royal Street as a front for trafficking virgins. It seems on one such occasion, a girl, Mary Fozatte, escaped and ran away but was consequently arrested "on charges of having stolen her own person, representing an estimated value of three hundred and fifty dollars." That was reported as the amount her virginity had been sold for, and Thompson felt owed that money. Rightfully, the court dismissed the case, and later the girl received fifty dollars in a court case in which she sued the madam for "character injuries."

Testing the waters on how far the prostitution gig for profit would be accepted was ongoing. Many a madam found herself in trouble with the law. The atmosphere was a breeding ground for violence, which often led to arrests. A newspaper article in the *Daily Item* on March 29, 1894, painted a further picture of the environment:

> *Last night at 8 o'clock a row occurred in Josie Lobrano Arlington's establishment, corner of Customhouse and Burgundy streets, between two colored servants named Emma Cutinez, alias Hill and Lizzie Jackson.*
>
> *The fight was the result of a game of craps between the two women and two waiters named Aleck and Harry. Emma won $65.75 and Lizzie squealed for her wealth. Because Emma would not give up, Lizzie hit her on the head with a spitoon inflicting a scalp wound.*
>
> *Corporal Seelhorst heard the row and arrested the women, the men escaping. The women were tried before Judge Ancoin this morning and were fined $25 or thirty days. Affidavits were made against the men.*

Some of the altercations were more colorful. Madams in all houses looked to entertain their guests in every manner of carnal pleasure. Some brought their creativity to new heights, leaning on the absurd. Animals were included in sexual performances that must have stunned the audience. On one occasion, monkeys were released from a house at 223 Basin Street and caused quite a scene, even biting a small child. On another occasion, the same house was visited by the board of health, which reported upon its inspection of the basement to have discovered "varieties of monkeys, trick

Malaria Makes Pale, Sickly Children.
The Old Standard Grove's Tasteless Chill Tonic drives out malaria and builds up the system. For grown people and children. 50c.

MONKEYS AT LARGE.

A negress named Jessie Brown, while on a bender, thought to have some fun by freeing two monkeys who were in a cage at her home, No. 223 North Basin Street. The frolicksome monkeys enjoyed their freedom by scampering through the streets, and ran to North Franklin Street, where one of them playfully bit Lena Hayman, aged 19 years, on the hand and arm, and also on the back of the head. Jessie was arrested, but the monkeys escaped.

Times-Picayune article, July 23, 1910. *Author's collection.*

ponies, and a general collection of animals which would do grace to a good-sized zoo." However, the report went on to state that the condition of the basement was in fine order and the animals well cared for.

Other times, prostitutes and sometimes madams took each other to court. Infamous madam Lulu White, a strong competitor of Josie Arlington's who ran the prestigious Mahogany Hall, often found herself in court. In one incident listed as "petty larceny," a news report states, "Constantine Cole, this accused was charged by a notorious White, with stealing a lot of valuable clothing." Apparently, an old dress and a Mardi Gras costume were found on the accused, who swore she had been given them to wash windows with.

In March 1899, a *Times-Picayune* article was published with the headline "The Wages of Sin" regarding a situation at the Arlington. "Shortly before two o'clock, Gracie Martin aged 25 years, a woman of the scarlet letter, in a fit of despondency, swallowed a dose of laudanum at Josie Arlington's establishment on Basin Street." Apparently, the woman received care at the hospital and was later reported in a condition out of danger. There must have never been a dull moment in the courts during this time. One can only wonder what the citizens away from Basin Street must have thought of the entire affair, in that it was a legal neighborhood of sin.

On yet another occasion, a colorful headline in the *Times-Picayune* read "Sam Hildreth Shoots at Hat, but Hits Dancer's Head." Also at Josie Arlington's house on Basin, a man known as a sharpshooter was dared by gaming man John Moses, who had been indulging with friends in champagne at the brothel, to show off his sharpshooting skills and attempt to shoot the hat right off Moses's head. Apparently, he aimed a little low, and "the bullet cut through the hat and ripped a huge [chunk] of fat off the head of the

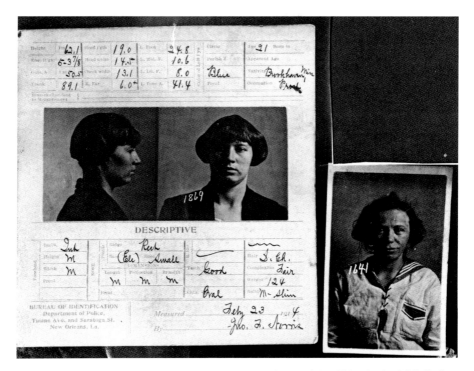

Typical prostitute arrest record. *Al Rose Collection–LaRC 606, Tulane University Special Collections, Howard-Tilton Memorial Library, Tulane University.*

alleged Mr. Moses." Hildreth went to his room and pretended to sleep. When the police got there, they shook him up and told him he was under arrest for shooting Moses, and Hildreth apparently let foul language fly.

The police, desperately trying to get to the bottom of the story, got no assistance from the head of the house, Josie Arlington, or her manager, Anna Casey, until threats were made by the police to take the women to jail as well. "They started to tell about Hildreth playing the William Tell act." Later, even though ambulance workers begged the wounded man to come with them to the hospital, he would not go, so they bandaged him up and left him there.

Most arrests made in that sector of the city were for physical altercations, with prostitutes fighting to hold on to their little piece of desolate pie. Josie, however, was often found in court along with her lover for having feverish altercations with each other. "The woman had for a number of years lived with the accused. They had numerous quarrels and were frequently before the Recorder's Court for fighting and disturbing the peace."

On one devastating evening during this time when rough and rowdy was the norm, Philip Lobrano came to the house and claims he insisted Josie not let her younger brother Peter in the house if he should arrive. Lobrano had had an altercation with a reportedly drunk Peter earlier at Louis George's saloon on Royal Street.

However, Peter did enter the house just fifteen minutes later at 11:30 p.m., and the two men had words. In a story published in the *Daily City Item* on January 29, 1892, it's reported that "Lobrano took a pistol from the mantlepiece [*sic*], and although witnesses attempted to prevent him, by getting between the two men, he shot Deubler." Lobrano shot Peter Deubler in the head. It was also reported that witnesses confirmed without contest that Deubler did not strike Lobrano, nor did he make a motion to suggest he was pulling a gun. However, as it turned out, the only people in the room at the time were Lobrano, Peter and Josie. There were no witnesses who jumped between them or attempted to stop the altercation.

Josie's account of the evening during her testimony in court was that she was in bed when Lobrano entered her room. She got up and got dressed, and when the doorbell rang, Mand Harris opened it for Lobrano. Josie met her brother in the hall and stated that Lobrano asked her not to let her brother in the room. The *Times-Picayune* printed an article following the trial

News Article - New Orleans Item (published as THE DAILY CITY ITEM.) - May 24, 1891 - page 4
May 24, 1891 | New Orleans Item (published as THE DAILY CITY ITEM.) | New Orleans, Louisiana | Page 4

THE DEUBLER MURDER.

Phil. Lobrano to Answer for Killing His Mistress' Brother.

The trial of Philip Lobrano, for the killing of Peter Deubler in the *maison de joie* of the former's mistress and the latter's sister, Josie Lobrano, at the northeast corner of Customhouse and Burgundy streets, on the morning of November 29, 1890, will be called to-morrow before Judge R. H. Marr in Section A of the Criminal District Court.

The woman had for a number of years lived with the accused. They had numerous quarrels, and were frequently before the Recorder's Court for fighting and dis-

The *Daily City Item*, May 24, 1891. *Author's collection.*

on January 29, fourteen months after the murder, in which it reported that Josie testified that "deceased did not insult Labrano [*sic*] when he entered the room. Accused said to witness, 'If he wants to keep the house, I'll go out.' Accused did not attempt to go out, and deceased did not strike him." She also testified that her brother did not pull back his hand as if to draw a pistol. "When accused called deceased a vile name, deceased stood up and said 'I'm not Phil; take that back!'" She said her brother rested his hand on the foot of the bed, and Lobrano went to the mantel, took his revolver and fired, using her shoulder to steady the gun. She further testified: "After the shot was fired I asked Phil what he had done, and his answer was that if I didn't look out he would shoot me."

Lobrano's testimony contradicts that. He stated that after he left Deubler, who had told him he was "going to raise hell!," Lobrano ran into John McGreevy, who told him that Deubler said he was going to kill him. He said he then went to Josie's and told her not to let her brother in. However, Deubler came, and when Josie let him in, "he came in the room and called me a ---- and said: 'I have got you.' I told Josie it was her fault, and he said it was his sister's house. I started out, and he said: 'No you don't you ----; I am going to kill you.' He threw his hand behind his back. After striking me, and I shot him, knowing that he was a dangerous man."

An ambulance took Peter to Charity Hospital and later to the Hotel Dieu, a Catholic hospital, where he was reported to have passed away two weeks later. During the court proceedings, Lobrano said Peter was known to carry a gun, although he was not certain that he had a gun with him that evening, but Peter had struck him, causing him to draw his weapon. However, witnesses, including Captain Donnally, stated that immediately after the shooting, the captain spoke with Lobrano and there were no marks on his face. Yet when Lobrano went to the police station the night of the shooting, he had a red mark across his face, which officers at the station confirmed. How the mark got there, no one knows.

Two witnesses, John T. McGreevy and William P. Ball, testified that "they saw Deubler a short while prior to the shooting. He was under the influence of liquor and made threats against Lobrano." Ball then found Lobrano and warned him.

Peter Deubler's mother-in-law, Elizabeth Hilroy, testified that Deubler, on his deathbed, confirmed that he was at fault and did not want Lobrano punished. However, Henry Deubler, Josie's other brother, testified that "I saw my brother the night before he died. He was then pretty bad off, and now and then was out of his head. At the time he knew he was going, and

LOBRANO ACQUITTED.

HIS SECOND TRIAL FOR KILLING PETER DEUBLER.

The State Introduced New Evidence—No Argument—The Jury Remained Out a Short Time Only.

Left: Caricature of Philip Lobrano in the *Times Democrat*, March 31, 1892. *Author's Collection*.

Right: Caricature of Peter Deubler in the *Times Democrat*, March 31, 1892. *Author's Collection*.

he told me that Phil Lobrano had shot him, and he asked me to promise him that I would prosecute Lobrano because he had shot him like a dog. This occurred in the Hotel Dieu, in the presence of Judge Hollander."

Philip Lobrano was eventually acquitted, and the relationship between him and Josie ended. When questioned regarding her relationship with Lobrano at the time, Josie did not answer. She did state that she had had relations with him for nine years, as well as other men, and that she had been to a ball just ten days after her brother's death (without Lobrano). "I have another man now," she said in court.

The entire affair of her brother's death exhausted Josie, who was about to begin the next chapter of her life with her new man.

Chapter 4

CRAFTY CREATURE

With the death of her brother and court case against her lover behind her, Josie felt the need to escape the city for a while. She headed to Hot Springs, Arkansas, accompanied by John Thomas Brady (aka Hearn). Brady was also a sporting man, and Josie must have felt good on his arm. Hot Springs was a resort town where the couple could relax and forget the past. And it seems that's exactly what Josie did. She left the past behind and began to plan for her future.

At the time, the most elaborate hotel in the town of Hot Springs was known as the Arlington. While the Arlington Resort Hotel & Spa still graces Hot Springs to this day, it is the third version of the hotel. The original version stood three stories high with the landmark twin towers and 120 guest rooms, giving it the status, at the time, of the largest hotel in the state. There was a grand courtyard between the two wings, and the elaborate rooms were illuminated by gas lights.

Josie was apparently fully impressed by the hotel, as upon her return to New Orleans, she announced that she would be changing the name of her house to Chateau d'Arlington. For six years, before opening the famous palace known as the Arlington, Josie worked to change her image and that of the brothel. No cursing was allowed inside the house, and she refined her persona, the rooms and her girls.

Seeking to appeal to a more sophisticated clientele, she recruited women who looked and sounded exotic. While she claimed they were imported from

Josie Arlington, circa 1910. *From the Josie Arlington Collection, courtesy Earl K. Long Library, University of New Orleans.*

around the world, the truth was she would recruit exotic women who had been circus performers or dancers to join her in New Orleans. She would then advertise the women as unique, exotic and refined. In fact, an issue of the *Mascot* from 1895 mocks, "Society is graced by the presence of a bona-fide baroness, direct from the Court of St. Petersburg. The baroness is at present residing at the Chateau Lobrano d'Arlington and is known as La Belle Stewart." Soon after, it was discovered that the woman was formerly from the Midway at the Chicago World's Fair, exotic as she was. However, time and time again, Josie's audience didn't mind the women's cover. Whether they were authentic or not was not the issue. The illusion was the allure; satisfying men's attraction to the mystery Josie had created was enough for her crowd.

The ruse worked, and Josie's brothel became very successful. She must have felt more comfortable in her shoes, masquerading as a refined lady who commanded respect. However, even in the more refined atmosphere, trouble would occasionally still come to pass in the house. The *Montgomery Times*, an Alabama paper, published an article on October 11, 1907, regarding a fight between two women in the Arlington, one of whom, Edith Douglas, eventually died.

> *The Douglas woman was an inmate of a house presided over by one Josie Arlington, in Basin Street. She became one of the "stars" of the establishment and, of course, the usual jealous envy was aroused among others of the same place. It is related that one night about two weeks or so ago a row occurred in the parlor of the Arlington place between Edith and another woman living on the premises. The combat was a fierce one and a blow was passed, but it is said that it was struck with the fist, the knuckles of the surviving woman landing on her rival's jaw and sending her to the floor.*

Douglas's death was investigated as a murder, as there was suspicion of a bottle being used to strike her, but all the witnesses of the house confirmed that her assailant only used her fist. The case was eventually dropped. So, while Josie desperately fought for respect and peace within her walls, the nature of the beast of her profession continued to interrupt her attempts at an elegant existence.

Regardless, Josie forged ahead and mingled with men in business and politics, opening doors for herself along the way. While no beauty, she is said to have had sex appeal. More importantly, she knew how to mingle among men, a unique trait that enabled her to discover opportunities and lead her business to success. It was very clever of her to position her house as one that only the finest gentlemen would frequent—a brilliant marketing strategy that would bring higher profits, put her in less danger and keep her in the circles of men who would provide her information regarding new legislation for the District.

Chapter 5

TOM ANDERSON

One can hardly discuss Josie Arlington without mentioning her unofficial business partner, Thomas Anderson. Business owner, politician, advisor to those in Storyville and watcher over the "District," Anderson was described by all as a likeable, in-charge guy who got things done.

Later known as the unofficial "Mayor of Storyville," Anderson was crafty himself. His entrepreneurial endeavors began when he was just a young newspaper boy, using his eyes and ears to help the police catch petty criminals. At the same time, he also quickly became a runner to select brothels, delivering cocaine, opium and whatever else they required. He learned the business from the bottom up and created opportunities for himself while working the neighborhood.

Anderson was not known to have a formal education, but his innate ability with numbers helped him secure positions with reputable companies, including bookkeeper for the Insurance Oil Company and the Louisiana Lottery, which was his entry to political connections in the city. His reputation and professional relationships led to him opening his first restaurant in the city in 1882. The Astoria Club on North Rampart Street catered to the circle of politicians, local businessmen and those of the underworld who could mingle and discuss business there in the casual setting.

In 1904, Anderson was elected as a member of both the Ways and Means Committee and the Committee on Affairs of the City of New Orleans, the latter of which he held for sixteen years. He balanced his political career and his business in Storyville magnificently for his purposes. His political

Tom C. Anderson, "Mayor of Storyville." *Courtesy New Comb Archives and Vorhoff Library Special Collections.*

connections served him well, as just a year before Storyville was established, he opened a restaurant—the Fair Play Saloon on the corner of Customhouse and Basin Streets—close to where the boundaries of the new red-light district would be drawn. He later changed the name of the Fair Play Saloon to Tom Anderson's. Josie and Tom must have found the connection between their two businesses beneficial, as later he added "Arlington Annex" as a tagline to the name of his saloon.

It is only speculation, but some believe Tom Anderson and Josie Arlington had a brief affair. While romance didn't last for them, if it even in fact occurred, they enjoyed a lifelong friendship and business relationship. In fact, when conversations of Storyville were in full motion, Anderson and Josie Arlington purchased property on Basin Street, which would be the premier rue of the new neighborhood.

Al Rose includes in his Storyville book that "the entire District was jocularly called 'Anderson County,' and city politicians recognized him as dictator of Storyville and dealt with the District through him. He settled internal disputes, punishing or rewarding, according to his own inscrutable principles." Anderson was, in fact, very protective over the District. He watched over the Tenderloin and defended it at great lengths. While working for the Record Oil Refining Company, he sent a letter to the current mayor of New Orleans, Martin Behrman, in which, after addressing a contract for fuel, he writes:

> *I also want to call your attention to the enclosed clipping in reference to the restricted district:—"They have begun this work as a result of the experience they have had in rescuing girls at the station, who, it is said have been on the point of entering one of the immoral houses, deceived into believing that they were respectable boarding houses." This I believe is a lie and believe they should be called down.*

No doubt, the city was trying to infringe on the District some moral clause that Tom wished to squash as quickly as possible.

THOS. C. ANDERSON,   FREDERICK NICAUD,   JOHN CUSHING.
        PRESIDENT.   VICE-PRESIDENT.   SECRETARY AND TREASURER.

| RECORD
AND
VENUS SAFETY
OILS. | | CYLINDER
AND
ENGINE
OILS. |

THE RECORD OIL REFINING COMPANY

INDEPENDENT
REFINERS OF

Petroleum and its Products.

REFINERY:
MELONIE P. O., ST. BERNARD PARISH.
WAREHOUSE AND DISTRIBUTING PLANT
ON L. C. M. R. GOVERNMENT YARD,
NEW ORLEANS, LA.
OFFICE: 517 GRAVIER ST.

ILLUMINATING, LUBRICATING
OILS AND GREASES,
GASOLINE, BENZINE.

NEW ORLEANS, LA.,   July 20, 1908

Hon. Martin Behrman,

    New Orleans, La.

My Dear Martin:-

        Received your letter and pleased to hear from you
and that Mauberret behaved himself and held up the honor of the fourth
ward while at Denver. Also pleased to note of your pleasant trip.

        Also want to say received proposal from the Sewerage
& Water Board for Fuel Oil. Will name our lowest price and hope between
you and the Senator will be successful in securing contract, having the
oil to carry same out without any trouble. Of course, would like to
know the last bid so as to be guided in quotation, but this being impossible will make best price possible.

        I also want to call your attention to the enclosed clip-
ping in reference to the restricted district:-"They have begun this work
as a result of the experience they have had in rescuing girls at the
station, who, it is said have been on the point of entering one of the
immoral houses, deceived into believing that they were respectable
boarding houses." This I believe is a lie and believe they should be
called down.

        Hoping you are well and enjoying the best of health,
I am,

                Sincerely yours,

Dic TCA

A letter Tom Anderson wrote to Mayor Behrman requesting support with corruption accusations. *Al Rose Collection–LaRC 606, Tulane University Special Collections, Howard-Tilton Memorial Library, Tulane University.*

In keeping with his industrious nature, Anderson also came to publish the *Hell-o* directory and later the *Blue Book*, a directory of District brothels and prostitutes within their walls. He printed the latter on the second floor of Lulu White's brothel on Basin Street once Storyville was in full swing.

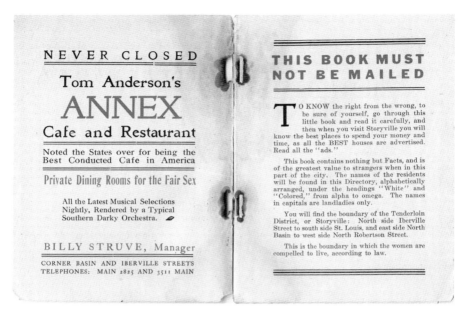

A *Blue Book* advertisement for Tom Anderson's Annex opposite a colorful brief description of the purpose for the guide. *Courtesy Newcomb Archives and Vorhoff Library and Special Collections at Tulane University, Collection NA-360.*

Yet another outrageous topping on the ever-celebratory New Orleans cake of festivities were the French balls known as the Ball of the Two Well Known Gentlemen and the CCC Ball. What better holiday to latch on to than Mardi Gras, the fest before the fast? Mardi Gras, "Fat Tuesday," of course is the last chance to indulge before Catholics trim down their vices and fast for Lent. Drinking, dancing, parading—anything goes. Festival balls are held throughout the city in conjunction with large parades such as Rex, Zulu, Bacchus and the list goes on.

Tom Anderson thus was the sponsor for Two Well Known Gentlemen, a sort of brothel field trip held at Odd Fellows Hall. The prostitutes, decorated in kitschy glam, hid behind masks and mocked the elaborate Carnival balls of the season. Like other Mardi Gras balls, they also chose a queen, but instead of debutantes carefully considered for each parade's ball, the scarlet women of the Tenderloin were plucked for royalty. Elaborate invitations were crafted, and hefty prices were placed on tickets. Many women in social standing couldn't resist the temptation to have a peek at the talked-about women of Storyville and the debauchery they represented.

A *Blue Book* ad for the "Two Well Known Gentlemen's" and the CCC Club Mardi Gras balls. *Courtesy Historic New Orleans collection Acc. no.1969.19.4.*

In 1906, several women convinced their husbands to secure them tickets and, hidden behind masks, attempted to glimpse the life of what the District offered. The intention of these social scoundrels was to get a taste of the perversion they belittled without putting their reputations at risk. To their chagrin, the cunning Josie Arlington got whiff of the ruse and crafted a surprise for the elite. She organized a raid on the ball with the police. The police were to search all women, and those present without proper paperwork proving that they were prostitutes in good standing were to be arrested. The fine women of the city were unmasked and sent home, but not before making an embarrassing stop at the police station.

It seemed all of it amused Tom Anderson, a man who liked to have fun. In an article in the *Daily Item* of December 24, 1901, he aimed to help his customers celebrate Christmas Eve:

> *Anderson's Fire Cracker—An Article That contains More Noise and Joy Than the Real Thing.*
>
> *Tom Anderson is passing out a Christmas present to his friends in the shape of a huge fire cracker. The fire cracker is of the regulation color, but it contains no powder or dynamite. What is in it, however, is calculated to cause much trouble, if taken in large quantities. Anyone who take enough of it would not mind walking through a street full of real cannon fire crackers in bare feet.*

Always out to show the sporting men in the city a good time, Tom was a man's man who appealed to the businessmen and women of the Tenderloin. He protected them and their businesses and seemed to be a real fair Joe. However, while those in the District counted on him, his reputation was not a favorable one in the general population. He was, in fact, greatly criticized for being protected by President Hayes and rescued when he should have been penalized for perjury and fraud in 1878.

Later, he was berated in many newspapers for his promotion of vices and the protection he continued to receive from the government. The *Colfax Chronicle* of July 31, 1908, takes aim:

> *New Orleans has been in the grip of a ring. No large city in the United States gets such poor returns for the public money expended as New Orleans. It is ill-paved, ill-policed, behind in municipal improvement; the public money is needed for a thousand and one sinecure jobs. By the same token, no other city of the country runs vice of every kind so wide open. Tom Anderson has been a great help. Highly prosperous himself, he has not failed to divide up with the power which enabled him to prosper; and he thus helped to make the saloonkeepers the gamblers, and the brothel keepers generous. It was his whim to go to the Legislature; and a grateful people, recognizing his services, rewarded him.*

A sarcastic poem was submitted and run in the *Louisiana Democrat* on March 27, 1878, regarding the fraud that was Tom Anderson and a direct complaint of his "being in bed with President Hayes":

"Tom Anderson, My Joe"
Tom Anderson, my joe, Tom,
When we were first acquent,
I bucked against your keno game
Till every red was spent.
Though I have quite reformed my ways—
For that was long ago—
It seems you haven't changed a bit,
Tom Anderson, my joe.

Tom Anderson, my joe, Tom,
Since then for many a year
You played a vastly meaner game,
In quite a different sphere;
A game at which the other side
Had not a chance to crow,
Because you marked and stacked the cards
Tom Anderson, my joe.

Tom Anderson, my joe, Tom,
When you began that game
I wondered that your throat was not
In danger from the same;
And when I passed a field of hemp
I smiled to see it grow,
And thought 'twas growing there for you,
Tom Anderson, my joe.

Tom Anderson, my joe, Tom,
You surely might have seen
That you, beside those Northern sharps,
Were very soft and green;
For when the game is politics,
So many tricks they know,
That they are quite too much for you,
Tom Anderson, my joe.

Tom Anderson, my joe, Tom,
They coaxed you on to sin;
They made you play a swindling game,
And racked the profits in'
They told you many, many lies,
And wept and pleaded so,
That you were badly swindled, too,
Tom Anderson, my joe

Tom Anderson, my joe, Tom.
You never thought that ways
Of wickedness were trodden by
The meek and lamblike Hayes,
Or that Ohio hands were made
To strike a sneaking blow;
But now you understand it all,
Tom Anderson, my joe.

Tom Anderson, my joe, Tom,
When you shall count the cost,
You'd better give away the game

At which you won and lost;
And you should well remember Hayes,
When you to prison go,
And not forget those other Frauds,
Tom Anderson, my joe.

In fact, Anderson was criticized in all circles outside the Tenderloin. It seemed he had not pulled the wool over the outside world, yet safe inside the red-light district, business went on as usual. In the *Crowley Signal* in November 1910, the paper takes a jab at other leaders in the city recognizing corrupt politicians instead of good men who should be honored. It uses Anderson as an example:

> *Why should the children be taught to honor failure, to remember a lost cause, instead of the wisdom worshiping success in the person of Tom Anderson, the tenderloin statesman who sells whisky to boys, as their fathers have honored him by choosing him as their lawmaker? And again, are not the red-light workers entitled to this honor for their political chief in return for their good work in confusing School Director Frantz as to his duties and swinging him over to the mayor?*

In 1910, after Josie retired and Anna Casey was manning the business of the Arlington, Tom Anderson met Gertrude Dix, a twenty-nine-year-old who entered the District, and the two quickly became an item. Dix managed many of Anderson's properties, and the two were eventually married.

Even in death, Anderson and Josie had much in common. Josie's brother Henry, upon learning that his sister had left the majority of her estate to his daughter and Josie's former lover, contested the will. Anderson's will was also contested under the same state concubinage law as was the case with Josie. However, Josie's brother had more legal grounds under that law. Anderson's daughter, Irene Delsa, must not have understood the law. It was proven in Anderson's case that he was in fact married to Gertrude Dix, now Mrs. Anderson, and the case was awarded to Anderson's wife, who generously granted Anderson's daughter half of the estate upon learning she was in fact his legitimate daughter.

Chapter 6

STORYVILLE

1897–1917

Storyville—the name itself conjures up an image of dames, drinks and debauchery. It was created by politician Sidney Story, officially on July 6, 1897, in an attempt to keep the seedier side of things in New Orleans contained to a regulated territory and out of the French Quarter. First labeled "the District" in reference to the red-light district, it was also known as "the Tenderloin" and, to Sidney Story's chagrin, Storyville, after the politician. While prostitution was corralled in the designated blocks, bordered by North Robertson, Iberville, Basin and St. Louis Streets, Storyville became a focal point of the city. Thirty-eight blocks of cribs—small rooms barely large enough to fit a cot—brothels and bars blossomed, keeping visitors to the city entertained. The train station near the area made it ideal for sightseers and visitors to access the unique neighborhood.

The nicer brothels—such as the Arlington, run by Josie Arlington, and Mahogany Hall, run by Lulu White—were also often frequented by politicians and New Orleans elite, who enjoyed meeting in the elegant surroundings for socializing and discussing business matters. In anticipation of the new neighborhood, their wise business sense spurred both Tom Anderson and Josie Arlington to purchase prime property on the main thoroughfare, Basin Street, which became the most iconic row of brothels in the District.

While the jazz music of New Orleans was not born in Storyville, New Orleans has Storyville to thank for giving the new style of music venues in which to flourish. Many of the musicians who later became famous, like Jelly Roll Morton and Louis Armstrong, played in the brothels and saloons

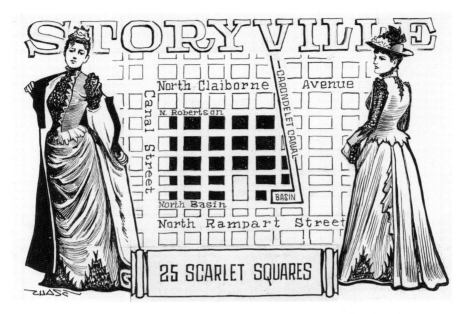

Above: This drawing by John Chase, a political cartoonist, reflects the Storyville boundaries. *Courtesy Historic New Orleans Collection, Acc. no. 1979-167.21a.*

Right: Sidney Story, creator of the ordinance to legalize prostitution in the neighborhood that carried his name. *Courtesy Historic New Orleans Collection Acc. no. MSS520.1916.*

50

Tom Anderson's Arlington Annex, the gateway to Storyville. *Hogan Jazz Archive Photography Collection, Tulane University Special Collections, Howard-Tilton Memorial Library, Tulane University.*

of Storyville, adding a great deal of entertainment and atmosphere to these locales. Like the fine décor in the Arlington and Lulu White's Mahogany Hall, the music was part of the foreplay that enticed so many to the brothels. The madams created such atmosphere that a visit to a house was an event. It was a fun experience on a variety of levels.

Like so many of the interesting attributes of New Orleans history, music is one that worked its way into the fibers of the culture. In the estate inventory of Josie Arlington (Mary Deubler's) succession, for purposes of establishing a value of the estate, the third parlor is listed as having "one piano," first on the list. Most of the Basin Street houses had either a conventional or a

A rare photo capturing all of Storyville, taken from a hot air balloon. *Al Rose Collection–LaRC 606, Tulane University Special Collections, Howard-Tilton Memorial Library, Tulane University.*

mechanical piano that took coins and could also be used with a "professor," or keyboard player. It is not specified if the Arlington's piano was mechanical, but to be sure, it was played by jazz pianists playing for tips. Customers who visited the houses were in good spirits and wanted to flaunt their wealth in front of their contemporaries and the ladies, so playing in a house on Basin Street proved to be a good income for the musicians who found their way there. It also brought them into circles other band musicians could not infiltrate. The piano was the instrument most welcomed into brothels, and it allowed black musicians to mingle with white customers, which was considered a luxury at the time.

Jelly Roll Morton, nicknamed for what black men called female genitalia at the time, was living the life. After almost turning down a guaranteed salary of one dollar a night, Jelly Roll rethought his future very quickly. He had been making fifteen dollars an hour "legitimately" and hesitated at even the idea of crossing through the District. But he was quickly shown the way via the opportunity for tips in any of the well-known houses. "Very often a man would come into the house and hand you a twenty, or forty, or a fifty-dollar note, just like a match." His attitude toward the District changed once he had a little taste. He noticed there were always police in the vicinity for protection, the atmosphere was more than festive, booze was pouring—good booze for that matter—and he was taking in more money than he had ever seen before.

Al Rose credits the biography of Jelly Roll Morton by Alan Lomax, much of which was in Jelly Roll's own words:

Storyville girl photo by Arthur Begou, depicting the glamourous side of the Tenderloin. *Al Rose Collection–LaRC 606, Tulane University Special Collections, Howard-Tilton Memorial Library, Tulane University.*

Jelly Roll Morton entertains brothel women, early 1900s. *Al Rose Collection–LaRC 606, Tulane University Special Collections, Howard-Tilton Memorial Library, Tulane University.*

All the highest class landladies had me for "the professor" if they could get me—Wille Piazza, Josie Arlington, Lulu White, Antonia Gonzales, Hilma Burt and Gypsy Schaeffer, the biggest spending landlady. Their houses were all in the same block on Basin Street, stone mansions with from three to seven parlors and from fifteen to twenty-five women, all clad in evening gowns and diamonds galore. The minute the button was pushed, that meant a new customer was in and the girls came in the parlor looking like queens. "Why, hello boy. Where you from?" Then I would hit the piano and when I'd played a couple of my tunes—"Got some money for the professor?" If the guests didn't come up with a dollar tip a piece, they were told "This is a high class place. We don't want no poor johns here." Matter of fact, no poor men could even get in these mansions. The girls charged high and made from twenty dollars to a hundred a night.

With the legalization of prostitution came a variety of other opportunities to profit. Small closet-like rooms, known as cribs, were constructed to optimize quick sexual experiences without any frills. Girls in cribs could be bought for as little as fifty cents a go. The prostitutes rented these cribs for around three dollars a night, allowing them to work at their own pace. Many of the girls who found themselves manning cribs were temporary transplants looking to make a quick buck during high season in New Orleans. The circumstances were so foul, as Al Rose writes: "Hoarse whispers from the doorways of cribs—'Half a dolluh, half a dolluh, half a dolluh, anythin' ya want fo' half a dolluh, mistuh'—would surely make many a man decide he wanted nothing so much as his privacy."

Josie Arlington moved into Storyville in 1891, temporarily running her small operation at 227 Basin Street, next door to the construction of what became her palace, the Arlington, at 225 Basin. There is only speculation that while on a long visit to Arkansas with her lover Tom Brady, the Arlington Hotel captured Josie's attention and led her to name herself and her brothel Arlington. From that moment on, she was driven to erect a structure so fine that it would be comparable to an elegant

Robertson Street cribs, condemned in 1939, were rented to prostitutes at three dollars a night. *Al Rose Collection—LaRC 606, Tulane University Special Collections, Howard-Tilton Memorial Library, Tulane University.*

Above: The river side of Marais Street from Conti to St. Louis shows "higher-class" cribs that offered inside plumbing, circa 1904. *Al Rose Collection–LaRC 606, Tulane University Special Collections, Howard-Tilton Memorial Library, Tulane University.*

Left: These simple cribs were tiny closets just big enough for a cot. *Al Rose Collection–LaRC 606, Tulane University Special Collections, Howard-Tilton Memorial Library, Tulane University.*

salon fit for a lady. Marble, wood and elaborate mirrors accompanied spectacular oil paintings, giving the lounges an elite atmosphere, so that the building itself became an attraction in addition to the entertainment the prostitutes provided. Josie commanded respect in what had been considered the most disrespected profession. This crafty creature turned the tables from what had been a somewhat scary and dangerous beginning to an extraordinary existence.

The section of the city that became known as Storyville was originally meant to keep the illicit conduct that was so prevalent in the city corralled to a manageable district and away from the general population. The act was meant to minimize the situation. However, Storyville became quite an attraction to the city of New Orleans and even a focal point. Even those who had no intention of partaking in what Storyville had to offer were glad to capture a glimpse of it from the train.

As a result of the legalization of prostitution, several brothels were transformed from seedy flophouses to jeweled palaces that rightly became the talk of the town. It became viable for madams like Josie Arlington to

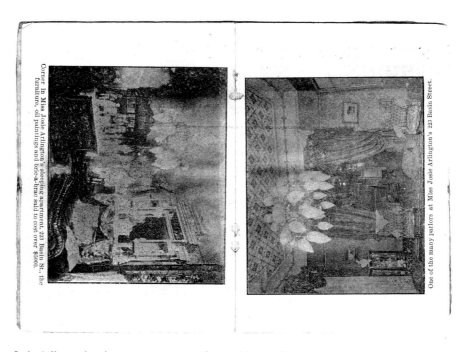

Josie Arlington's private apartment was featured in the *Blue Book*; the opposite page features the American Parlor in the Arlington. *Courtesy Historic New Orleans Collection Acc. no. 1969.19.4_010.*

A nice view of the American Parlor ready to welcome gentleman callers. *Hogan Jazz Archive Photography Collection, Tulane University Special Collections, Howard-Tilton Memorial Library, Tulane University.*

invest in their businesses and their buildings to create a flourishing industry. Josie took extreme pride in her furnishings and decorations for the Arlington, so much so that the house became a showplace where politicians and the bigwigs of the city felt comfortable socializing and discussing business. It was acceptable for men to meet there, insomuch as the vices there became secondary to the atmosphere.

As Josie advertised in Tom Anderson's *Blue Book*, she transformed the buildings into themed lounges so that customers could be transported into a variety of fantasies, including a Chinese Parlor, a Turkish Parlor, an American Parlor and an elaborate music and mirror room.

In 1905, another breakout of yellow fever hit Louisiana, resulting in the loss of 452 lives. However, in prior outbreaks no one knew what caused the disease. In 1900, it was discovered that mosquitoes were the culprits that carried and spread the disease through bites. An order was put into place to close all open sources of water. The order came complete with a fine to those who failed to comply. In an article by Laura D. Kelley, "Yellow Fever

The magnificent and costly Turkish Parlor at Miss Josie Arlington's, 225 Basin Street.

Corner in Chinese Parlor at Miss Josie Arlington's, only one here, 225 Basin Street.

Above: *Blue Book* pages featuring the Arlington's elegant Turkish Parlor on the left and the elaborate Chinese Parlor on the right. *Courtesy Historic New Orleans Collection Acc. no. 1969.19.4_011.*

Right: The Palaces of Storyville, featuring the Arlington's iconic onion-shaped cupola. *Hogan Jazz Archive Photography Collection, Tulane University Special Collections, Howard-Tilton Memorial Library, Tulane University.*

Basin Street, New Orleans, La.

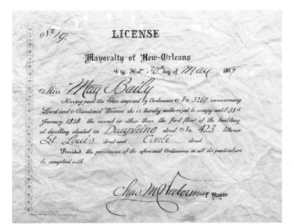

in Louisiana," she mentions that "this order went so far as to include the holy water receptacles located at the entrances of Catholic churches after Archbishop Placide Louis Chapelle died from yellow fever."

With yellow fever in addition to sexually transmitted diseases looming over Storyville, the madams in charge had to keep a close eye on the health of their prostitutes. While Storyville offered everyone a certain luxury to be open and free, there were these other evils that kept everyone from being careless. It was a remarkable time for women in particular. While the businesses the ladies of the houses ran may have been looked down on by those outside the Storyville borders, these women business owners were pioneers at the time.

The idea of living and working in a brothel might send shudders down your spine, but to be a fly on the wall is a different story. May Baily's to this day proudly boasts the establishment's original license on the wall. Until just recently, it offered guests a copy of a call girl license as a souvenir when visiting the bar, making it a tourist destination. Certainly, the novelty of what Storyville encompassed we will never see again. The idea of it both thrills and repulses. It's the ones who can see the gray between the black and white who might ache for it. The reputation New Orleans has worked for, been thrown into, has tried to crawl out of is a real melting pot of sweets and shit, stirred slowly. You either spit it out or crave more.

Only a small piece is left of the buildings that once sat proud on Basin Street, beckoning eager visitors to their doorsteps. Among the new condos that have been erected where the brothels once stood there remains a little corner store. A simple glimpse at what once was has escaped modernization— for now.

Chapter 7

COMPETITION, CAMARADERIE AND VOODOO

Prior to the establishment of Storyville, there was a smaller piece of the pie when it came to the pool of customers prostitutes had to profit from. The environment was rough, and the perception of prostitutes in general was gritty, dirty and dangerous. There are countless news articles of prostitutes being arrested for fighting among themselves, including the one of Josie's epic fight with Beulah Ripley. While fights among prostitutes continued even after Storyville was running, madams seemed to stay under the radar more. The news articles written about them changed from focusing on fights to business issues. There seemed to be a more civilized understanding among the women who ran the neighborhood.

Once the ordinance was in place, it allowed women who were creative to transform the profession in many ways. Josie Arlington and Lulu White were among the pioneers of smart and savvy women who changed the game, building palaces fit for kings so that engaging in paid sex suddenly turned from seedy to celebrated.

Over two thousand registered prostitutes worked the neighborhood at the pinnacle of Storyville's success. Once the famous thoroughfare called "Down the Line" was in place, a walk down the street from Canal would have introduced an interested person to two bars just before Customhouse (Iberville), the Terminal Saloon and the Frewclothes' Cabaret, but the first real welcome to the neighborhood was Tom Anderson's Saloon. As the train ran down Basin Street, tourists marveled out the windows at the attraction of gawdy houses and glitzy women flirting from windows, welcoming passersby.

The addition of the train, in fact, brought spectacular attention to Storyville, which was originally meant to be pushed out of the city, away from the eyes of respectable people. The focus of what could be considered "center city" changed drastically as the rail drove through Storyville, delivering travelers to the station not far away.

From Tom Anderson's it went Hilma Burt's, Diana and Norma's, Lizette Smith's, Minnie White's, Jessie Brown's, the Arlington, Martha Clarke's, Mahogany Hall and Lulu White's Saloon on the corner of Basin and Bienville. On to the next block were Frank Toro's Saloon, Countess Willie V. Piazza's, Antonia Gonzales's, Gipsy Shafer's, Emma Johnson's Studio, the Firehouse and Willie O. Barrera's. Small, modest houses sat between the palaces, and the architecture was as different as the services each house offered. The more elaborate houses offered games of chess and social time in the parlors, while more raunchy brothels like Emma Johnson's featured oyster dances (an oyster slip-sliding around a naked stripper who was able to maneuver it so that it wouldn't hit the floor) and foul sex acts for those with an appetite for the unconventional. There were "French houses" whose

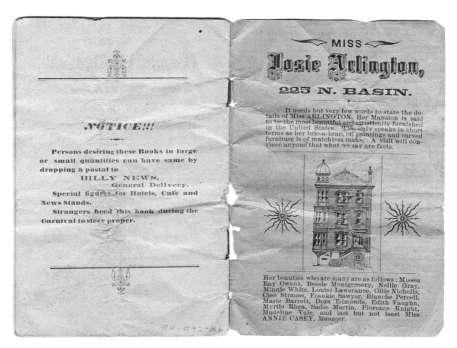

A *Blue Book* ad for the Arlington, highlighting Anna Casey as the manager. *Courtesy Historic New Orleans Collection Acc. no.94-092-RL_019.*

specialties were fellatio—a frugal positioning, in that it was the best use of the prostitute's time and space.

This brief run-down of Storyville brothels, taken from the website Storyvilledistrictnola.com, gives a snapshot of each brothel on the featured Basin and Iberville Streets, with the occupying madams throughout the brothels' history. It does not take into account the number of smaller houses and cribs behind Basin Street. The brief descriptions nicely follow the movement of madams from brothel to brothel and an estimated timeline of both the brothels and the madams running the houses.

209–11 Basin Street

1895–1900, under management of Flo Meeker
1900, passed to Hilma Burt; building was owned by Tom Anderson
1911, Gertrude Dix managed until the District closed in 1917

213–15 Basin Street

"French House" from pre-Storyville days to the closing of the District in 1917.
Prior to 1897, the octoroon Florence Mantley was in charge; she was succeeded by Yvonne LeRoy, then by Marguerite Angell, followed by Bertha Golden, who remained in charge until 1907.
1907, Diana Ray and Norma moved in and kept the establishment running until Storyville closed.

217 Basin Street

1895–1900, Antonia Gonzales occupied this address, followed by Gertie Sanford, Marie Denis and Lizzie Smith, respectively. Under Lizzie Smith, it was known as the Little Annex, which was the smallest house in the two blocks of Basin Street. (This property was also owned by Tom Anderson and used for his special guests.)

221 Basin Street

1894–1900, Nellie McDowell
1900–7, Ollie Nichols
1907–17, Minnie White

223 Basin Street

Until 1907, Grace Simpson (first president of Madams Benevolent Society)
1907, Jessie Brown's uninterrupted occupancy for seventeen years

225 Basin Street

1889, Josie Arlington (Mary Deubler), who had operated for some years at 172 Customhouse Street, built the Arlington mansion, which became the talk of the District. Josie retired in 1909.

1909, Josie rented the brothel to Anna Casey, her longtime manager, with Gertrude Dix as administrator.

227–29 Basin Street

Pearl Knight's house was located here until 1900.

1900, Gabrielle Michinard

1904–17, Martha Clark

235 Basin Street

About 1897, Mahogany Hall belonged to Lulu White, as well as the saloon next door. She operated her establishment until Storyville closed. This was the last Storyville landmark to be demolished in 1949.

307 Basin Street

Jeanette LeFebre, and afterward Frances Gilbert, except for briefly (approximately in 1915) when this location was operated by Rose Stein.

311 Basin Street

1897, it is speculated that Lulu White occupied this location while awaiting the construction of Mahogany Hall. When Lulu White moved into Mahogany Hall, Pauline Avery moved in.

1902–14, Ella Schwartz, followed by Bertha Weinthal until Storyville closed.

313 Basin Street

1880s, Dorothy Denning was madam (she also ran a house at 132 Burgundy Street). Lottie Fisher was in residence during pre-Storyville days until about 1904. Lillian Irwin operated the establishment for the following years of Storyville's existence.

315 Basin Street

Built approximately 1909 on property previously owed by Willie Piazza; May Spencer was the only occupant.

317 Basin Street

1897, believed to be a bordello run by Caretha Lopez and briefly Mamie Cristine.

Willie V. Piazza occupied this address throughout Storyville's existence.

319 Basin Street
Willie V. Piazza was here until 317 Basin Street was ready for occupancy.
When she moved out, Paulette Brian moved in until 1905.
1905–17, Camille Turner

321 Basin Street
Circa 1903, Egypt Vanita
1906, Violet Caddie
1917, Olga Lodi

325 Basin Street
Annie Ferris was in charge until 1906.
1906, Vivian Bonnaville was in charge until Storyville closed.

327 Basin Street
Rose Stein was involved in several ventures during Storyville's heyday. She
maintained this tiny house throughout that time.

331, 333, 335 Basin Street
Emma Johnson's French Studio. "The early days of Storyville found this
establishment too large for one occupant to manage, so it was partitioned
mid-way, with Ella Schwartz and Emma Johnson in No. 331. Marcel Nado
was in No. 335. Emma Johnson was able to take over the whole building by
1905 (until 1917), thanks to her 'sex circuses' and extreme bawdy activities."

341 Basin Street
Julia Dean operated this location until 1895
1895, Tillie Thurman
1904, Eunice Deering
1910–17, Willie Barrera

158 Customhouse (Iberville)
Hattie Hamilton. Hattie also operated the 21 South Basin Street establishment
and 184 Customhouse in the late 1870s.

166 Customhouse (Iberville)
Lulu White's first address of business in the District. Jessie Brown also was
madam here.

171 Customhouse (1547 Iberville)
1893, the Phoenix, owned by Fannie Lambert. "This was a large double building, and May O'Brien (on the other side) was in charge of the whole following Fannie's death (1904)."

172 Customhouse (1546 Iberville)
Original location of Josie Arlington's brothel.

1535 Customhouse (Iberville)
1863, Kate Townsend was in residence before she opened her house at 40 Basin Street. Notable madams were Antonia Gonzales and Gypsy Shaeffer.

The smaller houses probably appealed to those who were intimidated by the large, well-attended brothels, allowing a little more anonymity. Tom Anderson, in fact, kept a small house, Little Annex, tucked in the center of the block for carnal rendezvous for his most important and distinguished guests. Jessie Brown featured yet another marketing strategy. With the reported number of rooms exceeding sixty, volume was her plot. Maximizing even the slowest time, she offered a one-dollar special that included breakfast from 6:00 to 9:00 a.m.

Many more houses and cribs sat behind the iconic street, frequented by sailors who seemed to mostly stay away from the elaborate palaces. From the simple to the elaborate, there was a great deal of competition, yet the concentration of brothels, some of which were masterpieces of construction, brought an ease and charm to the neighborhood with an undeniable allure.

Josie Arlington, nicknamed "Queen of the Demimonde," and Lulu White, "Queen of Diamonds," as she wore diamonds on every finger, competed for the wealthy men who entered Storyville. Their palaces were comparable to one another with mirrored halls, fancy parlors and elegant private rooms with baths. However, Lulu had an added obstacle to circumvent with her quadroon status (one-quarter black). A flurry of laws popped in and out of her life, creating problems for the success of her brothel.

Quadroons, while highly sought after, were engaged in a most confusing game. White men could approach the mother of a quadroon and basically pay for her as his mistress. Once he found a suitable wife, he could toss the quadroon aside with no ramification and wed his white angel. However, many men kept separate houses and continued their relationships with their quadroons. Lavish quadroon balls were held, in fact, where young white men would seek out their mistresses, the beautiful women who had more

A *Blue Book* ad for the Arlington, depicting its exotic and elaborate parlors. *Courtesy Historic New Orleans collection Acc. no. 1969.19.4_012.*

rights than blacks but not all the rights of whites. It's not surprising that many of these beautiful women were enticed into Storyville.

Lulu White seemed also to be a bit more ruthless than Josie in her work ethic, as she was in and out of court for dealing in white slavery. While Josie held steadfast to never allow a virgin to be deflowered in her house, Lulu was less virtuous in that area, regarding it as great profit.

With the neighborhood ordinance that created Storyville there came the unfamiliar phenomenon of teamwork. Placing all houses together in the *Blue Book* was the first step to joint marketing. Bonding against the law and discussing business matters led to the creation of a group of Storyville women who met regularly.

Al Rose writes of several voodoo queens of New Orleans whom the brothel women were either terrified of or sought out to help their houses. He says they made a pact to not use the likes of a woman named Lala or, even worse, Julia Jackson, who was feared for her tremendous "sealing powder" that brought on a quick case of venereal disease that would end a prostitute's career. Jackson is said to have resided in the District, was six feet tall and cross-eyed. Women in the District who were not members of the "association" were said to threaten one another with hiring Jackson or Lala to curse their rivals.

Brought to Louisiana from Haitian exiles and predominantly West African captives, voodoo practices became ingrained in the Louisiana culture with spirit and ancestor worship. The practitioner's intense knowledge of herbal remedies proved valuable to local pharmacists who were intelligent enough to realize the natural remedies were successful. The pharmacists' sanction of various voodoo concoctions most likely gave some merit to the voodoo queens among the ladies in Storyville who often chose to enlist the help of practitioners with other problems. The creation of ritual charms and amulets for help with self-protection or harm to their foes was popular in Louisiana voodoo and shared in the brothels.

Congo Square, in what is today Armstrong Park, was the primary gathering place for early voodoo practitioners, and their drumming is credited as the birth of New Orleans blues and jazz music.

Eulalie Echo (Laura Hunter), Jelly Roll Morton's godmother, is said to have been one of the often-consulted voodoo queens in brothels and bars, creating elaborate potions to help those who hired her. Al Rose states that voodoo was the official religion of Storyville. Regardless of the prostitutes' true religion, they put their beliefs and hopes in the mysterious African spirituality. Marie Laveau, who became the most recognized voodoo queen in New Orleans, was in fact a devout Catholic. She thus must have been able to reassure those who enlisted her services that participating in voodoo and pagan rituals was not blasphemous.

Al Rose writes that prostitute May Spencer, a member of the "association," apparently feared that if the women of Storyville continued to toil in voodoo, they would draw the threat of the government closing down the District—a prophecy that proved true. However, the misconception and lack of understanding of the voodoo religion has led to its being greatly mischaracterized in countless reports and writings of the past. Most of the historical books written on New Orleans discuss the religion briefly and with a sarcastic tone and eventually reference the practices as trivial and a novelty.

Chapter 8

MENSTRUAL CYCLES, PREGNANCY AND VENEREAL DISEASE IN STORYVILLE

Women in Storyville had many challenges that have been alleviated by modern-day comforts since the late 1800s and early 1900s. However, when sex was your profession, one can only imagine just how much more womanly issues stifled everyday life. Prostitutes had to worry about downtime during "the curse," the imminent threat of pregnancy and a variety of sexually transmitted diseases.

A woman's menstrual cycle was a taboo subject at the time and something men avoided even talking about, unless it was a strange sexual fetish. Over the centuries, many strange misconceptions have been believed across cultures, such as that a woman during her cycle could turn meat sour or change the tide or that her blood could cause leprosy, among many other diseases. In fact, back to the time of the Bible in the book of Leviticus 15:19–23, there it is written:

> *When a woman has a discharge, and the discharge in her body is blood, she shall be in her menstrual impurity for seven days, and whoever touches her shall be unclean until the evening. And everything on which she lies during her menstrual impurity shall be unclean. Everything also on which she sits shall be unclean. And whoever touches her bed shall wash his clothes and bathe himself in water and be unclean until the evening. And whoever touches anything on which she sits shall wash his clothes and bathe himself in water and be unclean until the evening. Whether it is the bed or anything on which she sits, when he touches it he shall be unclean until the evening.*

No doubt men who visited Storyville were shielded from the monthly taboo and the women were either hidden away in an unused bedchamber or presented in a desirable fashion for fellatio. The cunning and driven woman would have temporarily focused on oral sex for income, most likely at the urging of her madam.

Menstrual cycles at the time are reported by the website Bloodandmilk. com to have been shorter and less regular, primarily due to malnutrition. The website references the article "Under Wraps: A History of Menstrual Hygiene Technology," by Sharra Vostral, as divulging that "menstrual blood was more of a novelty than a regular occurrence every month from about age thirteen to fifty-one."

Women would have worn something created in the late 1800s known as the "Hoosier sanitary belt." According to the website Medicaldaily.com, the belt was worn under a woman's clothes and used to secure washable pads. In 1888, the first disposable menstrual pads were introduced by Johnson & Johnson, known as "Lister's Towels." The website kilmerhouse.com explains that the product was marketed under Johnson & Johnson's "modesty-based" advertising approach and was the only category in its product listings that was printed with a large type heading. The advertisement for the towels tried to be discreet: "Lister's Towels, Sanitary for Ladies." However, women were too embarrassed to purchase the items in public, causing a continued marketing challenge for the company. In the document *Obstetrics: The Science and the Art*, Charles Delucena Meigs notes that he has "seen some, not a few women, who assured me they had never used any other precaution than that of putting on a thicker petticoat for fear of the exposure of their condition."

Pregnancy was an obvious concern in the houses of Storyville. There are, in fact, many references in countless books and articles to children being born and even raised in the brothels of Basin Street. The film *Pretty Baby* (1978), with Brooke Shields, theatrically exposes the topic as well as that of selling young girls' virginity and even the celebration thereof.

It's not clear if girls were made to wait until they had their first menstrual cycle before having their virginity auctioned off, but it's doubtful. The website bustle.com makes reference to a woman's average menstrual cycle beginning earlier with the coming of the Victorian era. "Known for its bone-crushing women's clothing and quaintly charming pornography—also represent the beginning of the downward slope in the age of women's first periods, from the high hit in the Renaissance." The website reports that a publication derived from a meeting of the American Gynecological Society in 1901 reported that they discovered that the average skewed down substantially from European women in the 1860s, at sixteen years of age and even older, to fourteen in Victorian girls.

It's further reported in a study by the same organization that those in the upper class began menstruation on average at thirteen and a half years old, compared to lesser classes beginning on average approximately a year later, noting nutrition as the primary cause. Consequently, a young girl who was put on the block in a brothel to relinquish her virginity most likely had not yet even began her first cycle.

At the time, there were surprisingly several methods of birth control available. However, the Comstock Law of 1873 made abortion and all forms of birth control illegal in the United States. Condoms, however, had been advertised since 1861 and even used by Egyptians since before 1000 BC. The new, much superior rubber versions were made possible through revolutionary innovations by the manufacturers of Goodyear tires. Condoms were even referred to as "rubbers" as early as the late 1800s.

Women also had the option of a contraption much like a diaphragm, called the "womb veil." Also made of rubber, it was inserted into the vagina to block sperm. Sadly, abortion remained a top option as a last resort. The website people.loyno.edu explains that while it was controversial and illegal by 1880, it was common through methods such as "surgery, poisons, home remedies, from plants and herbs, and mechanical means such as striking the woman's abdomen repeatedly."

Pregnancy and disease prevention were two of the major services enlisted from voodoo queens at the time. As herbalists, they may have been more successful than those who relied on old home remedies passed down or researched through the local pharmacist.

In 1914, Margaret Sanger, an activist for contraception, coined the term "birth control." She started the American Birth Control League in 1921, which was the forefather of today's Planned Parenthood. Regardless, children continued to be born in the brothels, and the girls often grew up to follow in their mothers' footsteps. The website infobarrel.com points to the story of a black Storyville child who recalls being initiated into prostitution at the age of eight years old, given the task of performing oral sex until her virginity was sold to the highest bidder at twelve, which led to a life of prostitution. While the facts in this particular story could not be verified, it is not farfetched to believe that several young girls born in brothels fell prey to a similar scenario.

Diseases were another motive for male customers to wear condoms. Venereal diseases—gonorrhea, chlamydia, syphilis—were all very present at

A *Blue Book* advertisement for a funeral parlor illustrates the power of the guide. Its circulation, while purely by hand, was widespread and considered valuable. *Courtesy Historic New Orleans collection Acc. no. 1969.19.4_008.*

the time but were not a consideration in the ordinance to contain prostitutes to the confined Storyville neighborhood. Alecia Long attributes the decision to Sidney Story not wanting to repeat a fight from women when mandatory inspections for venereal diseases were proposed in 1891. This action was tremendously opposed and fought by a highly influential group of women, and they ultimately won. Consequently, it was left to the inmates of the prostitution houses to protect themselves.

Chapter 9

THE *BLUE BOOK*

HONI SOIT QUI MAL Y PENSE

om Anderson's *Blue Book* was a fun celebration of the neighborhood. Meant as a tool for those visiting the city, the pamphlet highlighted all the Tenderloin had to offer. The book was published from 1900 until 1915. The moto of the book, known as "Order of the Garter," was *Honi soit qui mal y pense*—in French, "Shame on him who thinks evil of it."

The introduction to the *Blue Book* was colorful and did not change often; however, it was meant to capture the attention of the gaming gentleman and put him at ease for his carnal desires. An edition published in 1901 had the following introduction:

> *A man who wants to be a thoroughbred rounder these days has to carry a certain amount of hot air and be a wise guy, no matter how painful.*
>
> *Now if you are in the A, B, C class you want to get a move on yourself and "23," and to do it proper is to read what this little booklet has to say and if you don't get to be a 2 or 1 shot, it aint the author's fault.*
>
> *The contents of this book are facts and not dreams from a "hop joint."*
>
> *You will now find the boundary of the Tenderloin District commonly known as Anderson County or Storyville: North side Customhouse St. to southside St. Louis and East side N. Basin to West to W. side N. Robertson streets.*
>
> *This is the boundary in which the lewd women are compelled to live according to law.*

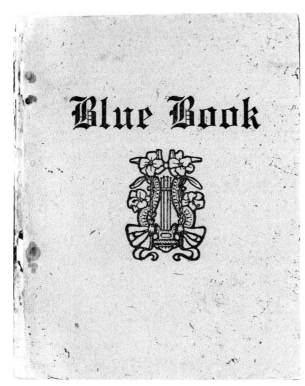

Left: The cover of the *Blue Book*, the guide to vice in Storyville. *Courtesy Newcomb Archives and Vorhoff Library and Special Collections at Tulane University, Collection NA-360.*

Below: A colorfully written *Blue Book* announcement justifying a legalized approach for paid sex. *Courtesy Newcomb Archives and Vorhoff Library Special Collections at Tulane University.*

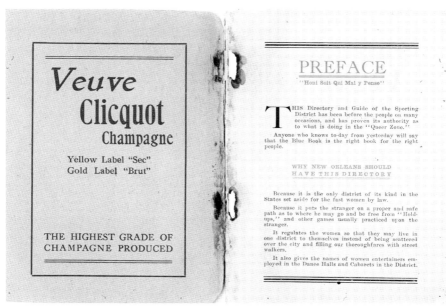

Veuve
Clicquot
Champagne

Yellow Label "Sec"
Gold Label "Brut"

THE HIGHEST GRADE OF
CHAMPAGNE PRODUCED

PREFACE
"Honi Soit Qui Mal y Pense"

THIS Directory and Guide of the Sporting District has been before the people on many occasions, and has proven its authority as to what is doing in the "Queer Zone."

Anyone who knows to-day from yesterday will say that the Blue Book is the right book for the right people.

WHY NEW ORLEANS SHOULD HAVE THIS DIRECTORY

Because it is the only district of its kind in the States set aside for the fast women by law.

Because it puts the stranger on a proper and safe path as to where he may go and be free from "Hold-ups," and other games usually practiced upon the stranger.

It regulates the women so that they may live in one district to themselves instead of being scattered over the city and filling our thoroughfares with street walkers.

It also gives the names of women entertainers employed in the Dance Halls and Cabarets in the District.

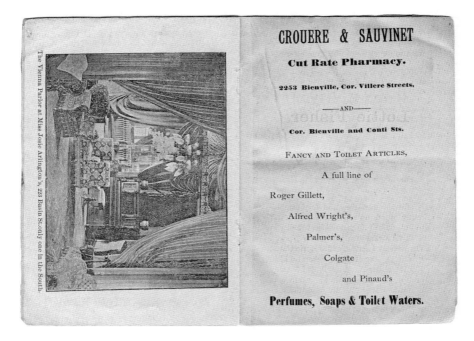

Above: The Vienna Parlor in the Arlington, alongside an ad featuring perfumes and toilet water. *Courtesy Historic New Orleans Collection Acc. no. 1969.19.4_13.*

Opposite, top: A *Blue Book* ad featuring the inside of Tom Anderson's Annex. *Courtesy Historic New Orleans Collection Acc. no. 2006.0237_28.*

Opposite, bottom: The *Blue Book* became a viable venue for businesses such as liquor purveyors and lawyers to advertise. *Courtesy Historic New Orleans Collection Acc. no. 2006.0237_002.*

Those who ran Storyville seemed to ignore those who were uptight about sex and instead advocated for a fun, relaxed approach to indulging and enjoying life's vices. It was a true celebration of sex for those willing to pay for it.

In addition to the brothels and saloons, other businesses found opportunity to advertise in the *Blue Book*, including liquor companies, attorneys and even funeral homes.

Today, the *Blue Book* serves as a look into the past with photographs of various brothel lounges and chambers. Josie Arlington took complete advantage of the book in which her brothel was highlighted. One ad boasts of her brothel, "No pen can describe the beauty and magnificence that reign supreme within the walls of Miss Arlington's mansion. The draperies,

carved furniture and oil paintings are of foreign make and a visit will teach more than a man can tell." The Arlington frequently took more pages than any other brothel in the book, with full-page pictures of the various exotic salons and even one image of Josie's private sleeping chamber.

The introduction for a book published in 1905 reads:

> *A Word to the Wise—The author of this Directory and Guide to the Tenderloin District has been before the people on many occasions, as to his authority on what is doing in the "Queer Zone"—Tenderloin. Everyone who knows to-day from yesterday will say that my* Blue Book *is the goods right from the Spring.*
>
> *Why New Orleans Should Have This Directory—First. Because it is the only district of its kind in the States set aside for the fast women by law. Second. Because it puts the stranger on a proper grade or path as to where to go and be secure from hold-ups, brace games and other illegal practices usually worked on the unwise in Red Light Districts.*

So, the book was positioned as the tool that would help a curious visitor find his way without cause to a pleasing situation. An additional page in the sixth edition of the pamphlet clarified its best use, explaining that the landladies or madams were listed in all uppercase letters. A capital *W* was placed in front of the names of all the white prostitutes, a capital *C* in front of all the colored women and "Oct" in front of all octoroons.

Interestingly, Josie very carefully positioned her ad not to reflect the beauty of her ladies but rather the beauty and sophistication of her palace, setting a tone for an elegant experience:

> *Nowhere in this country will you find a more complete and thorough sporting establishment than the Arlington. Absolutely and unquestionably the most decorative and costly fitted out sporting palace ever placed before the American public. The wonderful originality of everything that goes to fit out a mansion makes it the most attractive ever seen in this and the old country.*
>
> *Miss Arlington recently went to an expense of nearly $5,000 in having her mansion renovated and replenished. Within the great walls of the Arlington will be found the work of artists from Europe and America. Many articles from the Louisiana Purchase Exposition will also be seen.*

Brilliantly, Josie created an atmosphere of elite sophistication for her establishment so that those visiting would feel as though they were

Like the Stars above,

MISS

Olive Russell,

Of CUSTOMHOUSE ST.,

has appeared before the better class of sporting gentlemen of this community and never has her reputation been other than a highly cultivated lady. As an entertainer and conversationalist she has no equal; so when out for a good time don't over-look her house, her ladies are of a like character.

They are Misses Adele Richards, Ollie Young, Camile Lewis, Minnie Mc-Dohald and others.

MISS

Josie Arlington,
225 N. BASIN ST.

No pen can describe the beauty and magnifiance that reign supreme within the walls of Miss Arlington's Mansion. The draperies, carved furniture and oil painting or of foreign make and a visit will teach more than man can tell.

Her women are also beautiful and are as follows: Ollie Nicholls, Minnie White, Marie Barrett, Beach Mathews, Thelma Clayton, Myrtle Rhea, Frankie Sawyer, Madeline Vales, Freda Dunlap, May Spencer, Louise Ward, Florence Russell, Mate Gordon, Marie Cole, Amber Shippherd, Unice Derring and Madme Annie Casey. Manager.   PHONE 1888.

The Arlington

NOWHERE IN this country will you find a more complete and thorough sporting house than the ARLINGTON Absolutely and unquestionably the most decorative and costly fitted out sporting palace ever placed before the American public.

The wonderful originality of everything that goes to fit out a mansion makes it the most attractive ever seen in this or the old country.

THE ARLINGTON The Arlington. after suffering a loss of many thousand dollars through a fire, was refurnished and remodeled at an enormous expense, and the mansion is now a palace fit for a king.

Within the great walls of this mansion will be found the work of great artists from Europe and America. Many articles from various expositions will also be seen, and curios galore.

PHONE MAIN 1888

225 N. Basin

Above: An ad for the Arlington and its women. *Courtesy Historic New Orleans Collection Acc. no. 1969.19.4_009.*

Left: A nice descriptive advertisement in the *Blue Book* of what can be found in the Arlington. *Courtesy Newcomb Archives and Vorhoff Library and Special Collections at Tulane University, Collection NA-360.*

BLUE BOOK

TENDERLOIN 400.

Left: The *Blue Book* cover featuring the tagline "Tenderloin 400" was thought to be a mockery of socialite Lina Astor's four hundred socially acceptable people for her private balls in New York. *Courtesy Historic New Orleans Collection Acc. no. 1969.19.4_000.*

Below: This introduction to the *Blue Book* shows a sense of humor, directing people to "lighten up" when it came to Storyville. *Courtesy Historic New Orleans Collection Acc. no. 1969_002.*

SPEAK EASY HOUSES.

MRS. POALL, 1416 St. Louis.
LAURA LESLIE, 1418 Conti.
MRS. BARRON, cor. Conti and Treme.
REBECCA ALMICO, 1206 Conti.
CORA YOUNG, 1530 Bienville.
LUCY LAWSON, 1530 Bienville.
SALLIE FOSTER, 228 N. Robertson.
COOKIE BRIGGS, 1555 Customhouse.
ALICE WILLIAMS, 212 N. Robertson.
ISTIE MURRAY, 214 N. Robertson.
SARAH RUSSELL, 218 N. Robertson.
LIZZY CURTIS, 420 Howard, near Gravier.
GERTIE ROBERTS, 418 S. Howard.

THOSE WHO ARE STILL ALIVE BUT

ON THE Q. T.

ARCHIE CLARKE.
NELLIE ARMSTRONG.
TRILBY O'FARRELL.
LOUISE WINTERS.
GARNET RUINART.
ALMA BROWN.
JOSEPHINE CLAIRE.
IDA BRIGGS.
HATTIE THOMPSON.
PETRINELL BARR.
LILLIAN BLOODGETT.
LEE PERRY.
ELSIE FOSTER.
COMO LINES.

INTRODUCTION.

HOW to be WISE.

A man who wants to be a thoroughbred rounder these days has to carry a certain amount of hot air and be a wise guy, no matter how painful.

Now if you are in the A. B. C. class you want to get a move on yourself and "23", and to do it proper is to read what this little booklet has to say and if you don't get to be a 2 to 1 shot it aint the authors fault.

There is more than one way to spend your coin besides going against brace games and if you pay particular attention to this guide you will never be lead astray by touts or gold brick advisers.

The contents of this book are facts and not dreams from a "hop joint."

You will now find the boundry of the Tenderloin District commonly known as Anderson County or Storyville: North side Customhouse st. to South side St. Louis and East side N. Basin to West side N. Robertson streets.

This is the boundry in which the lewd women are compelled to live according to law.

☞**This Book not Mailable.**☜

experiencing a bit of culture in addition to a satisfactory romp. The *Blue Book* is a wonderful document that allows us a look into Storyville's cast of characters and the general environment at the time.

Another ad highlighted in the *Blue Book* was the Two Well Known Gentlemen Ball, hosted by Tom Anderson on Mardi Gras night. The ball was a spoof on the elaborate Mardi Gras masked balls and offered those with large pocketbooks an illicit evening of carnal entertainment away from the brothels. Anderson was very enterprising and took advantage of every opportunity to help Storyville flourish. The balls were heavily advertised in the *Blue Book* and were subsequently well attended.

Other similar pamphlets had also been attempted, but none was as successful as the *Blue Book*. Among them were the *Hell-o* and *The Red Book*, simply listing prostitutes and where you could find them. The *Blue Book*, however, had flavor.

While there were only five editions of the pamphlet published, tens of thousands of copies were printed and distributed throughout the city. They were conveniently handed out at the train station to arm gentleman visitors with the necessary information to guide them through Storyville. They were handed out for free at saloons and sold for a couple of coins at newsstands. The first edition was not slight, filled with 42 pages; however, the fifth and final edition was plump. First printed in 1912 and reprinted until 1915, the book had grown to 104 pages. Surely most copies found their way to the trash once they had served their purpose. Today, very few remain in existence, and they are cherished in libraries or private collections. Replicas are printed today by Applewood Books Inc. and can be found in souvenir and bookstores throughout the city.

Chapter 10

THE GREEN HOUR

ABSINTHE IN NEW ORLEANS

The great French wine blight in the mid-nineteenth century was caused by an aphid brought from America to France, most likely for experiments in vine grafting. However, the aphid destroyed French vineyards, as well as others throughout Europe. Wine became very rare and expensive, opening the door for a substitute: the green elixir absinthe.

Absinthe, an anise-flavored spirit, is traditionally light green, with the active ingredient being wormwood, an herb with thujone, that has been compared to have similar properties as THC in marijuana. The spirit has a very high alcohol content, as high as 148 proof, that is traditionally diluted with water when consumed. The alcohol's flammability contributed to the allure of the beverage, as it was incorporated into the presentation during the preparation of the drink. The absinthe is poured over a sugar cube to sweeten its innate bitter taste, and the cube is then lit on fire to caramelize the sugar for additional sweetness, creating a wonderful aesthetic effect.

With the absence of wine, absinthe captured the attention of had-been wine drinkers and gained a grand following throughout the mid-nineteenth century and into the early 1900s. The alluring green transparent liquid would swirl in the glass as water was dripped over the sugar. Eventually, the absinthe's reaction to the water changes the clear alcohol into an opaque concoction with a green tint. The drink was nicknamed the "green fairy," as the intoxicating liquid that was thought to have hallucinogenic properties also appeared to have fairy wings dancing in the glass during its preparation.

The mysterious green elixir that caused tremendous controversy in America and Europe flowed freely in the brothels of Storyville. *Courtesy Alys Arden.*

It became so famous in Paris that 5:00 p.m. became *l'heure verte*: the green hour. Only much later, when absinthe became banned due to misconceptions and the desire of the wine industry to regain its popularity once the "reconstitution" of the vineyards had transpired, did the green hour turn to what we now know as "happy hour." Later, those who ran the wine industry took advantage of the reputation absinthe had for its high alcohol content and use of wormwood, the "hallucinogenic," to attach a sordid reputation to the liquor.

In New Orleans, it was no different. Absinthe flowed freely in brothels and gaming houses. The use of it was frowned upon in the general population, which provided yet another reason to criticize those frequenting Storyville. An article published in the *Times-Picayune* was harsh:

> *The action of the drug which takes place with more or less rapidity according as the natural resistance of the victim to the craze is greater or lesser, is as follows: At first, following closely upon the loss of appetite, an unappeasable thirst takes possession of him, with giddiness, tingling in the ears, hallucinations of sight and of the hearing, and a constant mental depression and anxiety when not under the influence of the drug. Loss of brain power and either idiocy or furious madness shortly follow. The other, if more gradual, symptoms of the confirmed absinthe tippler are no less terrible. They begin with quiverings of the muscles and a great decrease of physical strength. Then the hair drops off, teeth become loosened in the gums; the absinthe drinker becomes emaciated, wrinkled and sallow-looking, and is a victim to horrible dreams and delusions of all kinds, and finally falls victim to paralysis.*

Drawing attention to the debauchery of the liquid was also pointing a finger at those who drank it. However, those caught up in the party palaces of Storyville paid others no mind. Madams were celebrities of sorts, and it was fitting that an exotic drink would be served in their houses. But newspaper articles continued to pop up chastising the drink and those who enjoyed it. A long article appeared in the *Vicksburg Evening Post* on October 12, 1912, explaining the evils of the drink and appealing to Washington to do something about the dangers of the green fairy: "It is this thing that constitutes the greatest danger of absinthe drinking—the utter indifference of the Absintheor to the dangers of the habit. He is in the same case with the man who has acquired the opium, morphine or cocaine habit—he does not care."

Absinthe. Its Abuse in France Becoming a Great - Times-Picayune - April 5, 1905 - page 10

April 5, 1905 | Times-Picayune | New Orleans, Louisiana | News Article | Page 10

ABSINTHE.

Its Abuse in France Becoming a Great National Vice.

Its Effects Deadly and Repugnant— An Increase of Tuberculosis Attributable to the Drug.

Says John N. Raphael in the London Mail: Frenchmen can no longer

Headline from the *Times-Picayune*, April 5, 1905. *Author's collection.*

Absinthe became illegal in 1912, primarily from the high pressure of the wine industry to snuff out the popular concoction so that wine could take its rightful place in the hearts of the drinking crowds.

In addition to indulging in absinthe, other, more dangerous vices infiltrated the city of New Orleans during these gritty times. Opium brought to New Orleans by the Chinese became a great evil. Most madams discouraged their prostitutes from visiting the opium dens, as those who ran the dens apparently offered the ladies free food in exchange for free sex.

The joints are as a rule the vilest kind of places, though they are one or two private establishments kept by others than Chinese, that are said by those who have been in them, to be as they are sometimes painted elegant with oriental splendor. These establishments are exclusive, however, but are as pernicious in their effects as the lowest of the ordinary joints. Anyone who has ever seen a confirmed fiend can readily recognize them in the streets and a close scrutiny and evening during a walk will reveal any number of men and women who have about them an abundance of evidence to show that they are a slave to the pipe and Chinese pleasures. Some effort should be made to suppress.

The city of New Orleans was in its young years of learning how to be bad, a reputation that it has continued to maintain. Absinthe, after ninety-five years in exile, was vindicated in 2007 and once again is legal in the United States to import, manufacture, sell and consume. It was learned that the liquor had been legal since about the 1960s. It was a misconception in the writing of the law that thujone, the active ingredient in the drink, had to be omitted. However, "thujone-free" apparently does not literally mean "zero thujone." According to the Wormwood Society, the information had been published and available since the 1960s, but it was not widely known. The "fudge factor" that constitutes the tolerance threshold was ten parts per million (10 ppm), approximately ten milligrams per liter. The loophole thus was established that absinthe truly only contains miniscule traces of thujone. It's also interesting to note that absinthe in the United States is for the most part exactly the same as that manufactured in Europe and is even imported from Europe to the United States. The Wormwood Society states that "it's been demonstrated by analysis that many of the alleged high-thujone faux absinthe products contain no more thujone than ordinary absinthe, and in some cases, none was detected at all. In some parts of Europe, marketing and labeling claims are not well-regulated."

Thus, our city with a somewhat seedy and sultry reputation can once again flaunt availability of the green fairy.

Chapter II

EVOLUTION OF THE
FRENCH QUARTER

The city of New Orleans, which consisted basically of the French Quarter until about 1862, had many challenges of its own beyond keeping prostitution at arm's length from respectable citizens. Yet as a source of income, city leaders were forced to balance what they believed to be a necessary evil. However, other forces were at play that would shape how the French Quarter would evolve.

By 1860, the city of New Orleans had taken on a new face. Emancipation had the affluent white families fleeing to Uptown to separate themselves from the poor and often desolate black families who were once their neighbors. Richard Campanella explains in his book *Bourbon Street* that when the boundaries between classes were "understood," downtown city life was agreeable to all. Small shotgun houses (a house with a hall that led straight from the front door through each room to the back door) occupied by poor working-class white or black families were tucked in between grandiose mansions, and each family's caste was defined. Suddenly, when free people of color walked the French Quarter streets for their own purposes rather than satisfying chores for their masters, the wealthy white families found coexisting as equals hard to stomach. The city now seemed to suffocate the wealthy white with its narrow streets filled with all races, mixed yet confused. Sharing the city space seemed impossible; thus, the affluent packed up and headed to neighborhoods that suited their self-worth and geographically segregated them from the riffraff. What is now the Garden District (named for its front and

A rare rooftop photo of Storyville, capturing the Arlington's majestic copula. *Courtesy Al Rose Collection–LaRC 606, Tulane University Special Collections, Howard-Tilton Memorial Library, Tulane University.*

backyards with gardens, as compared to the courtyards of the French Quarter) was their salvation.

Those who had formerly been slave owners found the transition next to impossible. Ann Wilkinson Penrose, granddaughter of famous general James Wilkinson, kept unsent letters to her son, a soldier, which served as a means for her to voice her resentment and anxiety with the changing times. Much like a diary, these letters are a treasure-trove of insight into past prejudice. The indignance of the aristocratic white breed during the time of emancipation is astonishing and difficult to digest. While blacks were learning to stand up for their rights, finding justice and separating themselves from what had been a hopeless and unthinkable existence, those who had enjoyed free-labor servants found the release and freedom of those servants unfathomable. Penrose writes in her letters, circa 1863:

> *February 2, Old Lyddy was here this morning, and very insolent indeed, telling Rebecca that she was free, and signifying she would do as she please, having previously used words to that effect, and even more insolent still to Kate.*

April 13, This morn. at breakfast, the bread was as usual intolerably bad, and as the flour is good it is the result of Becky, who is our cook at present; when the cakes came in they were also as bad as could be, heavy as lead, and like dough; I rose and went into the kitchen to speak to Becky; she was leaning down, with her back towards me as I entered, and I could not resist giving her a good hard slap on the shoulder, which bye the bye hurt my hand, I have no doubt, more than it did her, at the same time I asked her how she dared to send in such bread and cakes; she started up, looked furiously at me, and exclaimed, "don't you do that again, let it be the last time, or I'll just march out of this yard."

May 21, Clara had been most insolent and insubordinate to both yr aunts Vir. and Julia. Yr aunt V. took hold of her by her sleeve, I think, and attempted to slap her, whereupon she broke from her and ran screaming down the street, to a house about a square from this, which is the headquarters of some of the officers, and where there are always a number of negroe men in their service and uniform. There she laid a complaint, that she had been whipped with a cowskin, beat with a stick, and pitched down stairs. I was very uneasy knowing the consequences that have followed such reports, true or false, for they always take their side.

Not long thereafter, Ann Penrose left the city for Mobile, Alabama.

New Orleans found residents building homes in more exclusive parts of town, and with them went the fine stores and elegant hotels; even professionals moved their bureaus. Banks moved to Gravier and Carondelet Streets to begin the financial district, which later became known as the Central Business District (CBD), and the lovely ladies' boutiques followed suit. The Swamp had dissipated, with the brothel business flourishing on Gallatin Street, opening the environment for a successful business district to take root. City hall moved from the Cabildo to what is now Lafayette Square. The little village was being left behind as the city reached farther along the Mississippi and toward the lake. What were once quaint rues with hustling and bustling businesses and ladies walking to and from church, children chasing one another and buggies making deliveries became desolate and poorly kept underused dirty streets. Even the places of worship vacated to the more affluent neighborhoods.

Downtown had become crowded with half-class saloons and the type of people that those attract. Beggars, drunks and gamblers hung in and around the countless taverns, creating a sketchy environment and less than desirable atmosphere for respectable people to conduct what little business was to be done in what remained of the deteriorating town. Prostitution crept from the Swamp into the city that now welcomed it. And while octoroon women (one-eighth black), quadroon and black women were sought after for white men's pleasure, no black men were allowed in brothels. However, the light-skinned beauties who had been sex slaves when they were owned were now free women of color with still few rights. They often became mistresses sought out by young white men.

Property values declined, and the empty residential building thus became commercial, creating an even less attractive situation in the tiny neighborhood. What had been the vibrant center of the city became an outskirt, avoided by those who lived in New Orleans.

Finally, with the initiation of the Lorette Law, geographical boundaries for prostitution were put in place to curtail the limitless corruption of vice with hopes to pull in the reins and get a handle on the shifty and corrupt character that had oozed its way through the streets of the French Quarter. The aim of making prostitution "invisible" worked to push it toward the back of the neighborhood at Basin and Customhouse Streets. While that territory became corrupt and vile beyond imagination, it allowed breathing room for the French Quarter to reinvent itself. With the addition of the streetcars running down Royal and Bourbon, it became easier for people to travel within the city, and the growth of railroads brought travelers to New Orleans.

Taking advantage of the mighty dollar, new saloons, entertainment venues and hotels began to sprout up on Bourbon Street. Vaudeville-style theaters and circuses popped up along Bourbon, paving the way for concert saloons. These were more sophisticated than the outdoor variety shows and featured can-can girls who made a respectable living. While entertaining men with pretty women serving drinks and dancing, the concert halls were void of prostitution. Toward the late 1800s, a number of coffeehouses showered the Quarter, serving coffee and liquor. Businessmen, local and visiting, found the atmosphere agreeable to conduct business. As reported by Campanella, by 1897, the Underwriters Bureau of New Orleans documented that hundreds of guests were spending the night on Bourbon Street. Those who relished entertainment, but not carnal pleasure, got a kick out of passing by Storyville, gawking at the hussies in the windows, but they spent their time on Bourbon Street.

At the time, people were just beginning to travel for enjoyment with the onset of the railroads, and while they brought a great deal of attention to Storyville, they also brought travelers to the city of New Orleans, which began to build a personality for itself. Campanella further credits writers who took advantage of romanticizing the city and establishing a character for New Orleans that would eventually make it a destination for travelers, highlighting iconic buildings, Creole food and popular events such as Mardi Gras. New Orleans was, in fact, gaining a name for itself as a destination city, and tourists came seeking the sights they had read about.

Much in the same way that the affluent whites had fled the Quarter to avoid hobnobbing with the "trash" of the city, Josie found refuge in the comfort of her mid-city mansion around 1906, separating herself from the vice to protect her niece and attempt to capture the status for herself as that of a respectable lady. This was an interesting turn of events for someone who made her fortune in the neighborhood that continued to support her now lavish lifestyle.

As reported in Emily Epstein Landau's *Spectacular Wickedness*, oil baron and New Orleans businessman Santos Oteri made the comment that he must be forced to move out of his luxurious property due to houses of ill repute right under his nose. He felt vice should be corralled to specific neighborhoods and made no qualm about investing in what was a highly profitable business. He, in fact, owned six Basin Street plots that brought in high rent. But the "invisibility" of the business once again comes into play. Those in the city who moved in certain circles and considered themselves above the less fortunate who were clawing for each dollar didn't want to be reminded of vice when they were sipping their English tea with their grandchildren on their laps.

While Storyville for a time was a great attraction among all the other entertainment the French Quarter had to offer, its heyday came to an end. Around 1913, its reputation declined, and the area started leaning more toward the vice districts of the past: dangerous, deceitful and dirty.

Chapter 12

E.J. BELLOCQ

E.J. (John Ernest Joseph) Bellocq was a curious little man who is described in the queerest way possible in the book *Bellocq: Photographs from Storyville, the Red-Light District of New Orleans*, by Lee Friedlander, Susan Sontag and John Szarkowski. Szarkowski compiled a series of interviews in which various local New Orleans residents recollected their interactions with Bellocq.

New Orleans, and the French Quarter in particular, has always created "characters," and E.J. Bellocq was one of those. Dan Leyrer, a New Orleans photographer, explains that they used to call Bellocq "papa." "Not papa now, *papa*, because he was French you know and had a terrific accent and he spoke in a high-pitched voice, staccato-like, and when he got excited, he sounded like an angry squirrel. He talked to himself and would go walking around with little mincing steps. And he waddled a little bit like a duck, and he had this terrific head...."

Joe Sanarends, also a photographer and a former banjo player in New Orleans, joined in the "head" discussion with, "It looked like you took the head and squeezed it so it popped up about this high."

The amusing conversation about his head went on for some time, characterizing it as a "water head" with a detailed description regarding his very high forehead and his face widening at the bottom to create the effect of a pyramid. The image of a gourd comes to mind. Further, he was said to have been about five feet tall with narrow shoulders. Local musician Jonny Wiggs recalls, "He was short. And his sit-down place was very wide."

Rex Rose, in an article that can be found in the *Exquisite Corpse* at corpse. com, writes that upon Bellocq's death, "many almost mythic descriptions of him surfaced." He says he was described as "insane, hunchbacked, grotesque, dwarfish, or hydrocephalic, leaving the world with not much choice but to consider him a virtual New Orleanian counterpart to Toulouse Lautrec." However, Rose goes on to debunk the many references made to Bellocq's odd appearance. He explains that they are simple exaggerations from the imaginations of those who hardly knew him.

Regardless of what his contemporaries described as a most unusual physique, E.J. Bellocq was also characterized as always being polite and a bit of a mystery. "The impression I've had is that nobody seems to really know Bellocq," said Friedlander. Adele, one of Bellocq's models, recollects that he had taken countless photos, all of which she believed to have been very respectful, not "dirty." Yet while he had a great love for photographing women, he didn't seem to wish to engage in romantic interludes with his subjects. Rather, he admired them but couldn't be bothered by "knowing" them. He was intimidated or simply uninterested in anything but photographing the women.

Bellocq became the inspiration for the 1978 film *Pretty Baby*, in which somehow Keith Carradine was cast to play the part of Bellocq. The film, while very controversial, was in fact an honest look into a Storyville brothel and the man Bellocq might have been.

While Bellocq was in fact a professional photographer, his paid shots were mostly of real estate and technical photos of boat parts. A short article about him in a local publication, *The Owl*, included the only known photograph of him, depicting a young Bellocq not at all reflecting the contorted descriptions his peers had given, along with the following bio:

> *With pleasure we present a counterpart of the genial countenance of Mr. Ernest Bellocq, whose many good traits endear him to all with whom he comes in contact. After taking a classical course at the Jesuits college he devoted his space time to the pursuit of amateur photography and today ranks among the most successful and intelligent amateurs of our city, having been a prominent member of the New Orleans Camera Club, serving on the membership committee. The lantern slides contributed by him to the American Slide Interchange have been exhibited all over the world, calling forth much admiration wherever shown. The pictures illustrating the monuments of New Orleans were photographed especially for The Owl by Mr. Bellocq. He is a descendent of one of our most aristocratic creole families and has entrée to the most exclusive of social functions.*

The only known image of E.J. Bellocq. *Public domain.*

Rex Rose gives a brief background of Bellocq as having been born into an aristocratic white Creole family to Marie, "the daughter of a wealthy merchant from France," and father Paul, a French Quarter bookkeeper who later became secretary and treasurer for a wholesale firm. Ernest's brother Leo became a Jesuit priest, and Ernest completed ten years of formal education. At his father's request, he began a career in bookkeeping, which he eventually abandoned to his passion of photography.

His real estate photos paid the bills, but his love was photographing women and the seedy side of life. He was known to have taken countless photographs of women in brothels, as well as photos of the inside of Chinatown's opium dens on Rampart Street. It seems he enjoyed capturing the honest emotions of Storyville life. While luckily a small collection of the brothel slide negatives was recovered, sadly, none of the opium den photographs are known to remain in existence.

Bellocq was fond of women as a "subject" for his camera, and ultimately, capturing more than their sexuality on film was his gift. He took many photographs in which the prostitutes were fully clothed, portraying a mood in the finished work that evokes a solemn and melancholy emotion. He was very good at seizing the moment and was somehow able to convince many ladies of ill repute to bare all and pose for him time and again. Whether he paid them for their time or not is another mystery. They may have been flattered by the concept of modeling so that their egos saved him a dip in his pocketbook. It is believed that Bellocq took the prostitutes' photographs simply for his own use, not to profit in any way. It was indeed his passion.

That passion led to countless photographs, of which sadly only a handful of negatives remain—eighty, in fact. Those pictures tell the story of the Basin Street brothel inmates in their downtime, capturing who they were besides prostitutes—what moved them, what hurt them, what made them joyful.

Said to have had studios located at 840 Conti, 157 Baronne, 608 Canal and 818 Ursulines Streets, Bellocq spent his real photography time on-site at the various houses. Unfortunately, it's not clear in the photographs exactly where they were taken and which brothels were included, but it's likely he made his rounds.

There is a great mystery among some of the negatives that were recovered. If the allure of prostitutes captured on film for one single man's pleasure is not already completely fascinating, there later occurred a most unusual

Bellocq captures women during downtime at the house. *Public domain.*

phenomenon. Quite a few of the negatives had just the faces of the subjects in the photos scratched off. Some have speculated Bellocq's brother, who was a religious man, scratched them to protect the identities of the women. It could have been one of the prostitutes, one of the madams, someone else who found them much later or perhaps even Bellocq himself for some

Photo by E.J. Bellocq. *Hogan Jazz Archive Photography Collection, Tulane University Special Collections, Howard-Tilton Memorial Library, Tulane University.*

curious reason. We will never know how the negatives were "defaced." However, the effect certainly gives an eerie quality to the already unique pieces of art.

Rex Rose points out a suspicious situation during a Bellocq photo shoot. He explains that in one negative, a model is standing fully clothed in front of a large door. In another negative, she stands nude and her face has been

It's said that Bellocq kept these photos just for himself. Many of these are of the same woman, whose name was Adele. Photo by E.J. Bellocq. *Hogan Jazz Archive Photography Collection, Tulane University Special Collections, Howard-Tilton Memorial Library, Tulane University.*

scratched off, but more curiously, a couch has been moved in front of the door and a cord from an electric light has been used to secure the door, in addition to a lock that seems to be already engaged. It's true that in a brothel the use of secrecy for nudity is a very odd circumstance. One must wonder what they were hiding from.

A locket appears in several of the photographs of the women, and when Bellocq passed away, a locket was discovered in his safe deposit box by his father and brother, along with his mother's diamond rings, a rosary and a few other trinkets of jewelry. In his apartment, they apparently found among broken furniture and carelessly kept camera equipment the box of illegal pornographic negatives, which somehow found their way to Sal Ruiz's antique shop. They were later acquired by Larry Borenstein, who stashed them in an old dilapidated slave quarter bathroom behind Preservation Hall, which Rex Rose says was at one time photographer Pops Whitesell's studio. Whitesell also took spectacular architectural photographs around the

No one knows who did it or why, but several of Bellocq's negatives had the faces scratched off, adding an eerie dimension to the photographs of the naked prostitutes. *Public domain.*

Photo by E.J. Bellocq. *Hogan Jazz Archive Photography Collection, Tulane University Special Collections, Howard-Tilton Memorial Library, Tulane University.*

An iconic Bellocq photograph that has been featured in much print. This picture tells a thousand words. Photo by E.J. Bellocq. *Hogan Jazz Archive Photography Collection, Tulane University Special Collections, Howard-Tilton Memorial Library, Tulane University.*

French Quarter and New Orleans during the 1930s and 1940s. The studio's bathroom must have had a roof leak because several of the negatives were badly water damaged in Hurricane Betsy.

The plates were later acquired by Lee Friedlander, who printed them on period paper, creating remarkable versions that were shown at the New York Museum of Modern Art. Imagine how Bellocq might have gleamed at the notion of his afterlife success.

Those few who knew a little of Bellocq said he must have retired around 1938. Thereafter, he was known to walk about Canal Street with his Bantam Special hanging around his neck, attempting photos of streetcars and who knows what else might have captured his interest. The days of marveling at fallen women were then far behind him. It is a treasure that a few of his negatives remain to show us a glimpse into what Storyville once was.

Chapter 13

THE ARLINGTON FIRE

On December 1, 1905, around 11:00 a.m., while everyone within the Arlington had yet to wake after celebrating what might have been a grand Thanksgiving celebration the previous day (it wasn't until 1942 that Thanksgiving moved to the fourth Thursday of every November), the Storyville landmark was badly damaged by an electrical fire. It has also been speculated, however, that rather than a result of electrical failure, it is possible the flames were initiated by hired painters who were scorching the old paint off the building with intent to repaint.

The roof was completely lost, and the top two floors were badly damaged. However, a good portion of the ground floor was made of stone and was spared complete devastation. A *Times-Picayune* article, dated December 2, 1905, takes a jab at Josie, who seemed to have been calculating her options. "The losses and insurance on the building and contents were difficult to obtain on account of the different and contradictory statements made by the owner of the house." It seems that originally she claimed that furniture inside the house was worth $75,000 but that just a year prior to the fire she had purchased $25,000 worth of valuable paintings and bric-a-brac in Europe. This would bring the value to $100,000. Josie then added the cost of the building, which she reported she had paid for, but the $30,000 she submitted also included the land value. Later she changed her claim to $30,000 for the house and $25,000 for the furnishings. She also stated that she had been insured

Arlington Burned. Costly Storyville Palace Wrecked - Times-Picayune -
December 2, 1905 - page 5
December 2, 1905 | Times-Picayune | New Orleans, Louisiana | News Article | Page 5

ARLINGTON BURNED.

Costly Storyville Palace Wrecked by Mid-day Flames.

Rich Oriental Furnishings and Paintings Destroyed, Valued at $75,000—Grief Over a Mother's Picture.

At 11 o'clock yesterday forenoon, while all the inmates were yet asleep, fire was discovered in one of the palaces in Storyville, known at No.

Headline from the *Times-Picayune*, December 2, 1905. *Author's collection.*

for $65,000, but her insurance papers were in a box in the house, and she could not remember the name of the company at the time. The newspaper article goes on to state that the building only actually received about $3,000 damage, as only the top two floors were largely affected, and about $20,000 in damaged furniture and decorations.

The ladies in the house all found their way to Anderson's club, which was subsequently called Anderson's Arlington Annex. The *New Orleans Item* reported that "the inmates of the house, when they escaped from the burning building, assembled in Anderson's Saloon, at the corner of Customhouse and Basin Streets, but scantily attired." The women had been stirred from

Anna Deubler, niece of Josie Arlington and daughter of Henry, Josie's brother. *From the Josie Arlington Collection, courtesy Earl K. Long Library, University of New Orleans.*

slumber and left the house wrapped in sheets. Some managed to pack up their few valuables and belongings into the bedsheets and carried these bundles to Anderson's.

Josie is reported to have left her valuable jewelry in her private bedchamber on the fourth floor. "Special officer Scheffler was told by her where she had left the jewelry, among which was a diamond necklace which she valued at $1,500." However, Scheffler, once on the fourth floor, was unable to access the dresser where she had said the jewelry was. To protect any valuables, detectives were dispatched to keep a close eye on the building until everything could be retrieved.

The fire took the wind out from under Josie's sails. Many believe she was shaken by the thought of immortality and started from that moment on to live a very different life. The girls were temporarily housed at Anderson's Saloon, where they worked from the upstairs private dining rooms, but Josie's heart was no longer in the business.

In fact, a couple of years later she received a visit from Prohibition activist Carrie Nation. Known as "The Hatchet," Nation was relentless in her efforts to rid the world of corruption from vices. During Nation's visit in December 1907, according to the *Daily-Picayune*, Nation apparently prayed for the women at the Arlington, and Josie was reported to have told Nation that she was working to make more money so that she could open a home for unfortunate women—quite a turn for a madam. Nation's visit to New Orleans was a general hit. She preached from a table at Tom Anderson's and was reported to have said, "No indeed, I never did say that New Orleans was too bad for me to come to: No indeed."

Josie, meanwhile, had already began to build an alter ego for herself, primarily to protect what had become the focus of her attention at the time: her niece, Anna Deubler, the daughter of her brother Henry.

Chapter 14

THE TWO MRS. BRADYS

Demanding a good life for herself and her niece, Josie developed the habit of living two separate lives. While she was very fond of her two nephews, Josie felt especially protective over her niece, Anna. In fact, as far as we know, this was the primary reason she went by the name Mrs. Brady. She was adamant about hiding her business endeavors—while legal, they were less than desirable—from her Anna.

Over the years, Josie separated herself more and more from the brothel, staying at her first cousin Mary McLaffen's home on St. Claude Street, between Ursulines and St. Philip. Josie and her lover, Tom Brady, had meals from her kitchen brought to them so they could dine away from the madness. Josie's maid, Harriett Dumas, confirmed that often Josie and Brady wouldn't leave McLaffen's home until just before the Arlington opened at 8:00 or 8:30 p.m.

Harriett Dumas began working for Josie the day her brother was buried and worked for her until the day Josie passed. She recalls serving the two of them coffee in bed on countless occasions. Dumas often traveled with them to serve and look after them.

Josie had done very well for herself, and in addition to often donating money to the church, she and Brady lived the good life, playing husband and wife. They traveled frequently to Josie's summer home in Pass Christian. Josie had a place in St. Tammany Parish called "Anna's Villa," and she owned a farm in Abita Springs, where her nephew Henry Deubler Jr. tended to her cows, chickens and horses. He worked there from 1906 until his aunt's death.

Henry Deubler's son and daughter Anna as children. *From the Josie Arlington Collection, courtesy Earl K. Long Library, University of New Orleans.*

Her other nephew was named John Thomas Deubler, after Tom Brady, and the nephews called Brady "Uncle Tom." The fact that Brady was so much incorporated into Josie's extended family has one wondering why in fact they did not marry. Brady later said that he had wanted to marry Josie, but she chose not to. We will never know the truth.

The couple traveled to New York, Hot Springs, Cincinnati and several other places, in addition to taking Anna A. Deubler to school in Maryland. She first attended school at Dominican Convent in New Orleans and then the Convent Emmitsburg in Maryland. It was a life similar to that of any respectable family. In fact, Brady was the godfather of Henry's son John Thomas and Josie the godmother, which further illustrates her desire and dedication to living a well-respected lifestyle. Josie had apparently requested that those in her private circles and in their neighborhood refer to her as Mrs. Brady, particularly around her niece. It's possible most of the people they rubbed elbows with assumed the two had in fact married.

Her charade seemed to be going well, but a bump in the road came about when the sisters at the convent discovered Josie's profession and refused to allow Anna back to school. Then, sometime in 1902, the couple traveled to Europe and brought Anna to a convent in Paris. Josie was adamant that her niece would have the best of everything, even if she had to travel around the globe.

In 1906, Josie bought a mansion at 2721 Esplanade Street, where she and Brady continued playing house as husband and wife. They threw lavish parties and enjoyed life every bit as much as socialites of the city. Josie had manipulated her work to be quite separate from what went on at home, perfecting her double life. She balanced the two so brilliantly that she managed to keep up the charade for her niece for some twenty years, almost until the day she died. Other family members filled the Esplanade house, including Anna's parents and two younger brothers, enjoying Josie's support. Anna is said to have been her aunt's everyday companion. Alecia Long writes that "Anna and her aunt gardened, shopped for jewelry and hats, threw each other lavish birthday parties, had clothes custom made for themselves, and when they tired of the city, spent time at Anna's Villa in Covington."

In 1909, both Tom Anderson and Josie's lover Brady advised Josie to retire. She took heed and rented the Arlington to her longtime manager,

Josie Arlington's Esplanade mansion when it was located at 2721 Esplanade. *From the Josie Arlington Collection, courtesy Earl K. Long Library, University of New Orleans.*

A birthday celebration for Josie Arlington. Seated between her and Anna is Brady, and in the background on the right is Tom C. Anderson. *Al Rose Collection–LaRC 606, Tulane University Special Collections, Howard-Tilton Memorial Library, Tulane University.*

Anna Deubler in the garden at Esplanade. *From the Josie Arlington Collection, courtesy Earl K. Long Library, University of New Orleans.*

Opposite, bottom: Josie lived in this house with Tom Brady and her niece, Anna, far away from Storyville and the life that had made her image as the respectable Mrs. Brady possible. *From the Josie Arlington Collection, courtesy Earl K. Long Library, University of New Orleans.*

Josie worked hard to provide a lavish life for Anna, who never suspected her aunt to be anything but a respectable lady. *From the Josie Arlington Collection, courtesy Earl K. Long Library, University of New Orleans.*

Anna Casey, who is said to have done a very good job with the brothel. Meanwhile, in addition to living the life of a lady, Josie apparently reverted to her rougher past at times, as neighbors on Esplanade reported loud, angry behavior and a temper she had been known for in the past.

Josie fell ill sometime in 1913, and her dementia caused her to sporadically confide secrets of her past to Anna, who had become her nursemaid. Anna testified:

> *I think auntie was not herself. She was delirious, and she would say, "Little Girl, how I have been fooling you." And I would say, "You were fooling me very badly, very painfully indeed." And she would come out at times and would ask me what she had said. At times I would tell her and at other times I wouldn't, the things were too awful to repeat. I was very much astounded to hear auntie's life was such, and she told me she wasn't married, and told me the life she had been leading.*

While Anna was indeed foiled by her aunt and shocked, no doubt, it remains fact that Josie had created the elaborate scheme only to shield her dear niece from the illicit truth. Yet after her aunt's death, Anna seemed to feel owed all that her aunt had left behind. Perhaps it was the very laborious and less than charming job of caring for her aunt in the end that instilled a sense of entitlement in Anna, who was in fact the bearer of the greatest portion of the will.

Just prior to her death, Josie's state of mind had those around her plotting how to best secure her wealth once she had passed. Henry Deubler, her brother, recollects a phone call he received approximately two months prior to his sister's death that would change everything. "Mr. Brady rang me up at Vivian; he rang me up for me to come on home right away, and of course, I came home and as I got in the house my daughter said to me, well, she said 'I am going to marry Tom.'" He says she further justified "that we have everything our way fixed."

Henry explains in testimony that it troubled him greatly and that while at his sister's home, he and Tom would sit in the lounge and sometimes his daughter would enter and repeat, "Me and Uncle Tom are going to be married, whether you like it or not." He said that even on the day before they did get married, they wanted him to go into their room, and he refused. Henry was disgusted by the entire notion, knowing it was to be arranged for nothing more than to secure Josie's Esplanade property for Tom and whatever else of her estate was available.

Her father's anger seemed to grow regarding what seemed like an impossible situation. He faulted Brady for spoiling Anna over the years and told him to "take her," believing that he would also be disgusted by how spoiled she behaved—a sort of poetic justice for the two.

Josie Arlington, the once young prostitute, over the years had built her world into a small empire that now was in deep desire by those she left behind. In addition to the pages and pages of the succession that described in detail the furnishings and decorations in each room of the Arlington, her estate included shares in the Whipbro Oil Company and a long list of real estate, including 1: the Arlington, lot, building and all improvements bounded by Basin, Franklin, Bienville and Iberville; 2: two lots and all buildings and improvements bounded by Conti Franklin, Bienville and Treme Streets; 3: lot and all buildings and improvements bounded by Carondelet, Girod, St. Charles and Julia Streets; 4: lot and all buildings and improvements bounded by Canal, Cortez and Scott Streets and Cleveland Avenue; 5: lot and all buildings and improvements bounded by Broad, Columbus, Laharpe and Dorgenois Streets; 6: lot and all buildings and improvements bounded by Esplanade Avenue, Sixth, Lepage, Seventh and Washington Streets. All real estate came to a value of $53,200, a handsome sum at the time.

Josie passed away on Valentine's Day, February 14, 1914, at six o'clock in the evening. Brady told Henry the funeral would be a private event, and he would sell some of Josie's livestock to pay for the funeral. Newspaper headlines read: "Josie Arlington Is Claimed by Death—Body Interred in Tomb She Had Ordered Constructed."

> Josie Arlington, so-called "Queen of the Demi-Monde," is dead. People passing 2721 Esplanade avenue on Sunday afternoon saw a line of flower-freighted carriages winding to St. Boniface Church, where the last rites were held.
>
> In the group were two carriages of Sisters of Charity, two priests, two of relatives of the dead woman, and the others were filled with friends. There were eight altar boys and a number of orphans.
>
> The funeral was conducted by the Rev. Father Anselm Maenner of St. Boniface and Rev. Father Philip Murphy of the Jesuits. The dead woman received extreme unction a few days ago.
>
> Among those attending the funeral were Mike Rooney, Thomas C. Anderson, John T. Brady, Judge Richard Ostero and others.

News Article - New Orleans Item (published as THE NEW ORLEANS ITEM.) -
February 17, 1914 - page 2
February 17, 1914 | New Orleans Item (published as THE NEW ORLEANS ITEM.) | New Orleans, Louisiana | Page 2

JOSIE ARLINGTON IS

CLAIMED BY DEATH

Body Interred in Tomb She Had Ordered Constructed.

Josie Arlington, so-called "Queen of
the Demi-Monde," is dead. People passing 2721 Esplanade avenue on Sunday
afternoon saw a line of flower-freighted carriages winding to St. Boniface

Headline from the *New Orleans Item*, March 17, 1914. *Author's collection.*

Strange to say, though her life had been spent among the women of the demi-monde, none attended the funeral. The only homage received at the hands of her companions were wreaths of flowers sent to the home and laid upon the tomb.

Josie is reported to have donated a great deal of money and land to the church throughout her life; thus, even with her questionable profession, she was welcomed among the Jesuits.

In 1911, preparing for her final parting, Josie met with Albert Weiblen Marble and Granite Company Inc. to have a brilliant and unique tomb created for her. It was made of rose marble and granite and included a

Plans for the original tomb constructed by Albert Weiblen Marble and Granite Company Inc., which are currently housed in the Tulane University Architectural Archives. This version shows the name "Brady" carved into the granite. *Author's collection.*

brass statue of a woman knocking on the door of the tomb. The statue held a bouquet of roses in the other arm. Many believe the statue was meant to represent the virgins who knocked on her door, whom she turned away. Josie prided herself on having never let a virgin be deflowered in her house. Yet her family, as well as Harnett T. Kane, author of *Queen New Orleans*, make note of another idea for the statue's symbolism. It's possible the statue was erected to represent the very night she was turned away at her family door after missing curfew and knocked but rather was turned away, which led to the life she both endured and enjoyed.

Many different amounts for the sum Josie paid for her tomb have been listed in print; however, it is documented that she paid $5,500 to have the tomb constructed in 1911, a handsome price. She signed the paperwork herself and was seemingly very involved in having it created. The original title was for plot no. 5, and the tomb was later moved to plot no. 13.

Albert Weiblen was a very prestigious company and took its tomb plans very seriously. Its customers were paying a great deal of money for peace of mind when they passed. Some tombs at that time cost as much as $40,000. The company would produce small models of the tomb, as architects would do for high-priced buildings for their clients. It is not known if one of these models was created for Josie's tomb, and it probably wasn't, but several of these models still exist in the Tulane University archives. Currently stored in the athenaeum among filing cabinets and historical documents, these models were created in the 1800s and early 1900s and

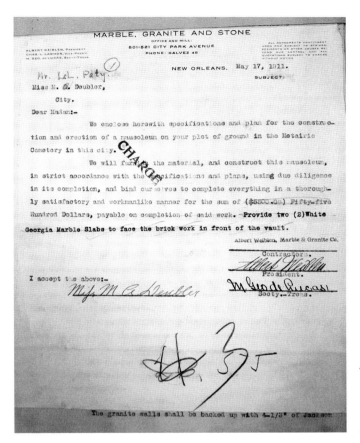

The contract from Albert Weiblen Marble and Granite Company Inc. for the tomb Josie had built in 1911 clearly shows the invoice amount for $5,500, a grand sum at the time. *Author's collection.*

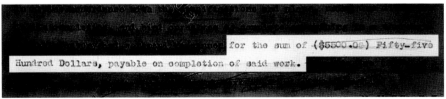

Mary Deubler's signature on the contract for her tomb. The contract is housed at the Southeastern Architectural Archive, Special Collections Division, Tulane University Libraries. *Author's collection.*

Hidden in the Southeastern Architectural Archive of the Howard-Tilton Memorial Library at Tulane University, safely stored away from danger of being damaged, are these little treasures. These tiny tomb models were produced prior to their larger versions, the majority of which were constructed to be housed in the Metairie Cemetery. *Author's collection.*

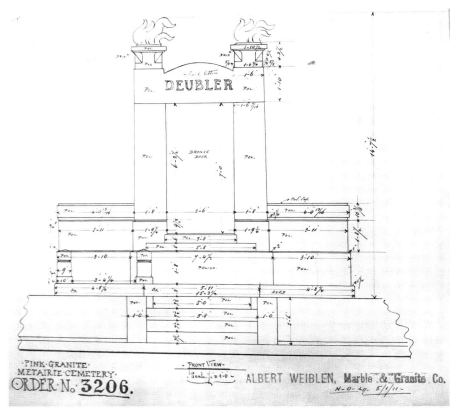

The original plans of the tomb, created by Albert Weiblen Marble and Granite Company Inc., remain in pristine condition in the Tulane University Architectural Archives. This version shows the name "Deubler" carved into the granite. *Author's collection.*

are in perfect to near perfect condition. Just another little treasure chest from New Orleans's past.

Several illustrations of Josie's tomb were created in the early stages of its inception. One plan has the name "Brady" carved into stone, and the other reads "Deubler." In fact, on the contract for the tomb, prepared by Weiblen, the original document has typed in, "Governing the material and erection of a granite tomb to be erected in Metairie Cemetery for Miss. M.A. Deubler of New Orleans, La." However, the "Miss M.A. Deubler" is crossed out in pencil and handwritten in as "Mrs. Brady." Although Brady is reported as saying to Henry that he wanted Josie buried under the name of Mrs. Brady, it seems Josie decided the tomb

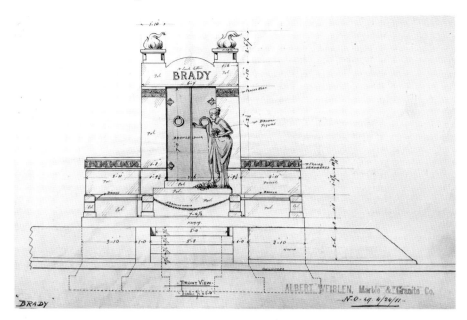

Here the plans have been changed to show the name "Brady" carved into the tomb, an option Josie had originally considered. *Author's collection.*

should sport her family name, as an article from the *New Orleans Item* on February 17, 1914, reads, "Only one word, 'Deubler,' is carved upon the shaft. It was her maiden name."

Chapter 15

THE WILL

On February 19, 1914, just a few days after Josie's death, a search was ordered for her will, as published in the *New Orleans Item* article "John T. Brady Petitions Court for Action." Apparently, a will could not be found. However, Brady pleaded that he believed Josie left a will and that he was the executor. Brady believed the will to be in her safe, to which no one knew the combination. An order was made to have the safe opened, wherein the will was found. Brady was in fact confirmed as sole executor of the will.

A recap of the will listed the following:

Contents of the premises No. 225 N. Basin St. (the Arlington)	$3150.00
Notes (jewelry, titles to tombs in the Metairie Cemetery)	1600.00
Real Estate	53200.00
Cash	1247.00
Equal to the total amount of this inventory	$59197.86

Meanwhile, Anna accompanied Brady to an attorney on February 21, exactly one week after her aunt's death, where she signed papers securing the Esplanade property in Brady's name. Later, they returned to the Esplanade home, where they were married. The rush was no doubt to accommodate them in securing the home on Esplanade, which Josie had made prior arrangements with Brady to receive. However, he had never finished filing the documents, which was necessary in order to secure the property in his name. As published in the *New Orleans Item*: "Conveyance

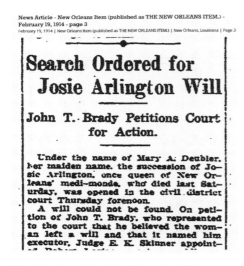

News Article - New Orleans Item (published as THE NEW ORLEANS ITEM.) - February 19, 1914 - page 3
February 19, 1914 | New Orleans Item (published as THE NEW ORLEANS ITEM.) | New Orleans, Louisiana | Page 3

Search Ordered for Josie Arlington Will

John T. Brady Petitions Court for Action.

Under the name of Mary A. Deubler, her maiden name, the succession of Josie Arlington, once queen of New Orleans' medi-monde, who died last Saturday, was opened in the civil district court Thursday forenoon.

A will could not be found. On petition of John T. Brady, who represented to the court that he believed the woman left a will and that it named him executor, Judge E. K. Skinner appoint-

Headline from the *New Orleans Item*, February 19, 1914. *Author's collection.*

records indicate that the acquiring of the property by Mr. Brady was by a gift or other transfer made claim by Josie Arlington during her life-time. At her death Anna Deubler went before a notary, relinquishing all rights to either property or movable contents of the home." Since Josie made it clear in her will that Anna was to receive the lion's share of her belongings, the house would have reverted to her as well. However, now that they were married, Anna relinquished her claim to that property.

Henry continued to be aghast at his daughter's plan with Brady and filed a lawsuit contesting the will. Even though Josie had bequeathed him three plots of land, it wasn't enough, and he had found a legitimate complaint. Since Josie and Brady had lived in open "concubinage," there was a viable issue with the law. In the court document "Argument for Henry Deubler, Plaintiff," it is stated:

> *The law provides that persons occupying towards each other, the relations, which J.T. Brady and the deceased in this case, has been proven to have occupied are incapable of making to each other, whether* inter vivor *or* mortis causa, *any donation of immovables; and if they make a donation of movable, it cannot exceed one tenth part of the whole, value of the estate.*

Thus, the games began. Henry was relentless in his efforts to foil his daughter's plan. Headline after headline filled the newspapers with the case: "Brother Attacks His Own Daughter to Strike at John T. Brady," "Charges Also Niece Committed Acts That Forfeit Her Right to Heir," "Brother Attacks Josie Arlington's Probated Will," "Josie Arlington Money Stirs War."

However, Henry had a point; it was a significant mess. The court document states, "If ever there was a case of open concubinage this case presents it." Meanwhile, it also remained a fact that a document dated January 13, 1913,

News Article - New Orleans Item (published as THE NEW ORLEANS ITEM.) -
March 1, 1914 - page 1
March 1, 1914 | New Orleans Item (published as THE NEW ORLEANS ITEM.) | New Orleans, Louisiana | Page 1

J. T. Brady Now Owns Josie Arlington Home

Wife, Former Anna Deubler, Relinquishes Her Claims.

The home of the late Josie Arlington, 2721 Esplanade avenue, valued at
$25,000, has become the property of
John T. Brady.

Anna M. Deubler-Brady, niece of

Above: Headline from the
New Orleans Item, March 1,
1914. *Author's collection*.

Right: Headline from the
Daily Picayune, March 17,
1914. *Author's collection*.

Josie Arlington Money Stirs War Brother Attacks - Times-Picayune (published as
The Daily Picayune) - March 17, 1914 - page 12
March 17, 1914 | Times-Picayune (published as The Daily Picayune) | New Orleans, Louisiana | News Article | Page
12

JOSIE ARLINGTON MONEY STIRS WAR

Brother Attacks His Own Daughter to Strike at John T. Brady.

From left: Brady's brother's wife; his brother, John T. Brady; and Anna Deubler surrounded by John's brother's children. *From the Josie Arlington Collection, courtesy Earl K. Long Library, University of New Orleans.*

stated that Brady had paid Josie $25,000 for the house; he had simply never completed the legal filing.

Henry also made a claim to jewelry that was in the house, listed as one Lavellier (a pendant with dangling jewels), one locket and chain, one diamond bar pin, six solitaire diamond rings, one marquise ring, one sunburst, one diamond crescent pin, one diamond bracelet, one pair of diamond earrings, two small rings and two bracelets. However, the probate document also states that "said jewelry was given by the deceased long previous to her death as a manual gift to her niece Anna Deubler, and the said jewelry is now in the possession of the said Anna Deubler. Proving otherwise surely would have been impossible.

The court eventually ruled for Brady and Anna, whereupon Henry filed an appeal on September 20, 1915. The court, after dragging niece, nephew, housemaid, cousin and a large cast of other characters back to court as witnesses, again ruled in favor of Brady and his new wife, Anna.

Anna, thirty, and Brady, fifty-one, consequently lived as husband and wife in what was once the Esplanade home of Josie Arlington, the woman

The large cement slab that was moved along with the mansion at 2721 Esplanade Avenue to 2863 Grand Route St. John. *Author's collection.*

The mansion Josie once lived in, later moved to 2863 Grand Route St. John, remains at that location to this day. It was renovated around 1978 by realtors Don Goudeau and Larry Suchand. *Author's collection.*

who had supported and spoiled them all. The couple had no shame in the surreal situation that one can only imagine Josie would have found difficult to stomach. Josie is said to have told her corset maker once that she dreaded the day Anna would marry because "men are such dirty dogs." To discover her beloved niece had betrayed her would most likely have left her devastated.

Unusual circumstances continued to follow Josie even in death. The Esplanade home was in the section of the city where plans were underway to build a school. In 1922, the city gave Brady and his wife ninety days to decide whether they would like to move the home to another location. They chose to have it moved just a couple of blocks away to 2863 Grande Route St. John, where it remains to this day. The cement block with the Esplanade address carved into the cement was moved with the home and still sits outside the home on the curb. The McDonogh City Park Academy #28 remains in the former location of the mansion.

Chapter 16

THE GHOST OF JOSIE ARLINGTON

On February 15, 1915, Josie Arlington was removed from her tomb at the wishes and directive of Mr. and Mrs. Tom Brady, and the tomb was eventually sold, coincidentally, to "J.A." Morales. Josie's remains were thus placed in another undisclosed location in the cemetery. This option, thankfully, is no longer a viable one per the cemetery. In fact, at this time, no individual whose God-given right to remain in the tomb they had purchased prior to their death can be removed from it by anyone, unless it is an upgrade or there is an improvement to the original tomb.

The law/tradition of events occurring a year and a day after a death seems to originate from many beliefs and has subsequently been adopted as a recognized legal time frame for a variety of circumstances, including lawsuits and burial rights. In pagan religion, the time frame is recognized as the duration of the temporary handfasting wedding ceremonies, until a clergyman to officiate the union can be secured. In an article written in the *New Yorker* by Edwidge Danticat in January 2011, he explains the significance of a year and a day in vodou or voodoo:

> *In the Haitian vodou tradition, it is believed by some that the souls of the newly dead slip into rivers and streams and remain there, under the water, for a year and a day. Then, lured by ritual prayer and song, the souls emerge from the water and the spirits are reborn. These reincarnated spirits go on to occupy trees, and, if you listen closely, you may hear their hushed whispers in the wind. The spirits can also hover over mountain ranges, or in grottoes, or caves, where familiar voices echo our own when we call out their names.*

Current view of what was once Josie Arlington's tomb, now belonging to the Morales family. *Author's collection.*

Regardless, Josie Arlington/Mary Deubler only remained in the tomb she had built for that short duration—the tomb where she believed and desired to remain for eternity. While the Bradys claimed that they were selling the tomb due to the heightened amount of attention it was receiving, it was more plausible that they sold the tomb for money. Darlene Brocato recalls the situation being looked on with disgust by her family. Josie had taken care of her entire extended family in one way or another—employing some, offering donations to others—but Brady and Anna benefited the greatest from Josie's wealth. The fact that they would even consider selling her tomb showed a level of greed that is difficult to stomach. They waited the exact legal time that a body had to remain in a tomb before being moved under the City of New Orleans guidelines—one year and one day. Josie had taken

Rear view of the tomb that once sat facing Old Pontchartrain Boulevard, at the point called "Dead-man's curve." *Al Rose Collection—LaRC 606, Tulane University Special Collections, Howard-Tilton Memorial Library, Tulane University.*

care of everyone to the point it seems they lacked the wherewithal to know how to take care of themselves after her death and looked to her aid one last time, stripping her of all she truly had left.

The tomb she had built in 1911 is said to have had a strange aura around it from the time it was placed in the Metairie Cemetery, even prior to Josie's death. A groundskeeper swore that before Josie's body was placed in the tomb, it burst into flames one evening while he was keeping watch. Others have claimed to have also seen the tomb's flame aglow and even the statue turning toward them and then walking from the tomb and into the grounds—a romantic notion for sure.

Several years after the tomb was in place, a railroad sign pole was placed on the road outside the cemetery, which had an unusual effect. The red light caused the tomb to light up red and flames to glow. In *Queen New Orleans*, Kane writes, "Even after death red lights for Josie....Thousands gathered every night. As a youth I watched with them, and I can recall the eerie effect, the frightened exclamations." While it is difficult to believe that "thousands gathered every night," the cemetery confirmed that the tomb became a problem for traffic outside the cemetery, and it was consequently moved to plot thirteen, where it stands today.

The website Moonlit Road (themoonlitroad.com) highlights the story as well:

> In the years after Josie was buried, rumors began to spread about strange goings-on at her grave. Curiosity-seekers who visited the grave ran back to town claiming they saw the urns on top of the tomb burst into flames before their eyes! Others saw an eerie red glow coming from the tomb at night, as if the granite walls were burning like hot coals. Josie's grave was soon nicknamed the "Flaming Tomb."

Kane shares a further interesting anecdote that one morning the statue went missing. Imaginations in the city went as far as to conclude that it had come to life and walked about the grounds. However, it was apparently recovered in a nearby trash heap. He claims it was then restored and returned to the tomb. While his story from *Queen New Orleans* could not be verified, it would make sense that the theft of the tomb led to the legend of the statue roaming the cemetery grounds.

While the tomb now belongs to the Morales family, many still refer to the iconic memorial as the tomb of Josie Arlington.

Whether the catalyst for Mary to begin her life in the business of sex was her parents' refusal to allow her back home, her choice as a stubborn

German girl to make a go of it on her own, she was guided into it cunningly by her then lover Philip Lobrano or a combination of all three, the woman who transformed herself into Josie Arlington became a legend. She threw herself into a man's world and clawed herself to the top to end up holding the reins. From a party girl to a woman who surrounded herself with the finer things in life, she was remarkably strong. The people she loved and cared for enjoyed the life she provided and seemed to be helpless without her. Raise a glass to Josie, the woman who helped tame a rough world.

Chapter 17

IN CONCLUSION

Why memorialize a prostitute? Now that we have a clearer picture of who Mary Deubler was, we can decide if we can learn lessons from her, respect and even idolize her, be entertained by her, feel compassion for her, be understanding of her or be disgusted by her, but we certainly can't pity her. She was a woman who, in a truly "man's world," took the bull by the horns, learned, listened and then constructed her Storyville.

She was turned away at an impressionable age and seemed to have let those impressions guide her into a world of sin and debauchery. So few choices were available to a young woman in the 1800s. When a woman with a strong will and mind was thrown into a hungry New Orleans, whether forced or tempted into independence by her own stubborn accord, there were certainly few options for survival. Guided by a lover who had little scruples, she seemed to have learned in spite of herself and in a reasonable amount of time that violence was not the way to a comfortable survival.

The woman who soon called herself Josie Arlington built an empire that supported her family, friends and lovers. She was an intricate piece of a diabolical puzzle. She grinned at the cunning men who pulled the strings, and occasionally she was able to cut a thread to curtail the path in a direction toward a better life for herself and her family. They call prostitution the oldest profession in the world, but Josie and her contemporaries helped women reap the rewards of their labor. These women ran the business that had before them been manned by masculinity.

Literature romanticizes Storyville, creating an atmosphere many find enticing and alluring. "Oh, to be a fly on the wall!" In her heyday, Josie Arlington was able to bring fantasy and eloquence to what had been a dirty and disgraceful lifestyle. Her parlors were glitzy, the girls glamourous and the entertainment enchanting. However, surely the girls who worked in the houses of Basin Street went from nights of being regarded as celebrities to having men who owned them for the hour demoralizing them, leaving them crying into their pillows and perfume.

While the champagne and money were flowing within the walls of the Arlington, Josie had a bigger plan. She bought property, hired family to run her estates and traveled. She bought a lavish mansion and went shopping and dining with her beloved niece. Yet her strong business sense and entrepreneurial nature couldn't obtain her the respect she longed for. She was a woman who had infiltrated a world that laughed at women, lusting after them but devaluing what they brought to the table. She wanted respect. The noble women of New Orleans shunned the likes of her, but Josie did not bow down to their prejudice toward the vice their husbands welcomed.

Had Josie followed in her mother's footsteps, what might she have been capable of? There is very little known about her parents or even what her father's profession was. Might she have married into a noble lifestyle, raising a respectable family? We can only wonder, as Josie must have now and then imagined, as she sipped a lemonade on the porch of her Esplanade mansion. Her brother and his family took residence there, and her lover, who "worked" by her side, reaped the rewards of what she had created.

Regardless, she left behind a legend. Josie Arlington is mentioned in countless books and documentaries on the topic of New Orleans history. She gave the finger to all who tried to control her, and she seemed to create for herself the life she desired. Even after death, those she loved took advantage of what she had created. Sadly, it seems she never found true love—or did she?

Afterword

LOST BUT NOT FORGOTTEN

While researching information for this book, I became very fond of Josie Arlington, recognizing how important she truly was to New Orleans's culture and history. When I discovered the original plans of the tomb she had created in 1911, which are currently housed at Tulane University Architectural Archives, I studied them intently. I imagined Josie meeting with Albert Weiblen, together designing her tomb with intricate details. The three-page contract describes in precise details the excavations, footings, brickwork and granite, as well as the bronze statue "to be life size and will be [fastened] with bronze lag screws as it can be moved aside when required and easily replaced." I pictured her explaining how she wanted the statue to look and what it meant to her. She must have been thrilled when she was presented with the option of rose granite, a style that certainly suited her: rare, sultry, brilliant and designed to make a statement.

I imagined her debating which name to place on the front of the tomb, and I was surprised that Deubler had won. I believe Josie knew it was to her advantage to have a man at her side, but I don't believe she ever found true love. Perhaps Brady loved her, but I believe the true love of her life was not a romantic one. She took her niece under her wing and wanted to give her everything she never had. It was disheartening for me to discover that the same niece later, once Josie was deceased, made decisions her aunt certainly would not have been joyful about.

Removing Josie from her tomb—an option the cemetery has confirmed is no longer a possibility—was clearly not what Josie had wished for herself.

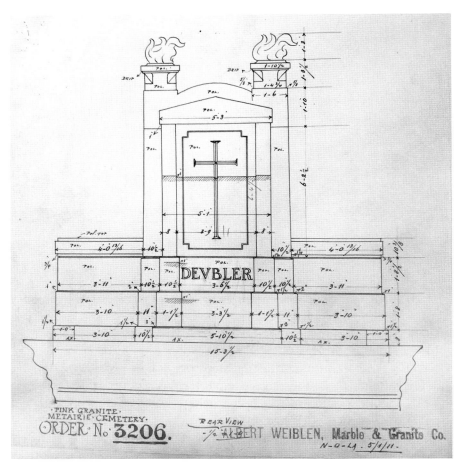

Plans of the tomb showing the cross that was placed on the back. *Author's collection.*

Whatever the circumstances were that led her niece to remove her aunt and sell the tomb we will never know. Some say it was due to the tremendous amount of attention her tomb was attracting, while others believe Anna and Brady sold it to pay bills. However, the decision went against Josie's obvious wishes, with no means to defend the act.

One afternoon, while looking over the old tomb plans all spread out on my large round table, I became melancholy as I marveled at my luck of discovering their existence at Tulane University. Then it hit me like a ton of bricks. I had an idea. I contacted Darlene Brocato, Josie's descendant, on a rainy New Orleans day and proposed the idea that we put Josie back into her

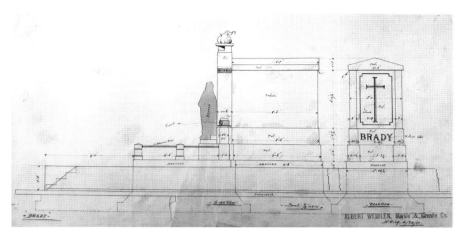

Side view of tomb, showing intricate details. *Author's collection.*

tomb. Darlene found the concept inspiring, and we immediately planned a date to meet at the cemetery to discuss the necessary measures to organize what would become a monumental task.

Indeed, we found there are several hurdles to overcome, including a court order, along with many important decisions that will be necessary along the way. It is certainly no easy feat to accomplish. However, her family believes it to be the right one, and I believe Josie would feel honored and appreciative to again rest in peace as she had intended.

Thus, the author portion of the proceeds for this book will be donated to do just that. Until Josie Arlington is back in a granite tomb, as close as possible to the specification she desired, each book that is sold will contribute to the funds necessary to make that happen. We will be forced to make small concessions for financial reasons, but we will let what we believe to be decisions Josie would have agreed with guide us. I am proud and honored to be able to do this for the woman who was Josie Arlington, an icon in New Orleans history.

BIBLIOGRAPHY

Asbury, Herbert. *The French Quarter: An Informal History of the New Orleans Underground*. Garden City, NY: Garden City Publishing Co. Inc., 1936.

Brandt, Allen M. *No Magic Bullet*. Oxford, UK: Oxford University Press, 1985. Repr., 1987.

Campanella, Richard. *Bourbon Street: A History*. Baton Rouge: Louisiana State University Press, 2014.

Epstein, Emily. *Spectacular Wickedness*. Baton Rouge: Louisiana State University Press, 2013.

Fortier, Alcee. *A History of Louisiana*. Vol. 1. N.p.: First Rate Publishers, 2016.

Huber, Leonard V. *New Orleans: A Pictorial History from the Earliest Times to the Present Day*. N.p.: American Legacy Press, 1971.

Kane, Harnett T. *Queen New Orleans, City by the River*. New York: William Morrow & Company, 1949.

Kemp, John R. *New Orleans: An Illustrated History*. N.p.: Windsor Publications, 1981.

Leavitt, Mel. *Short History of New Orleans*. N.p., 1982.

Long, Alecia P. *The Great Southern Babylon: Sex, Race, and Respectability in New Orleans, 1865–1920*. Baton Rouge: Louisiana State University Press, 2004.

Meigs, Charles Delucena. *Obstetrics: The Science and the Art*. N.p., 1852.

Powell, Lawrence N. *The Accidental City*. Cambridge, MA: Harvard University Press, 2013.

Rose, Al. *Storyville, New Orleans*. Tuscaloosa: University of Alabama Press, 1974.

Schafer, Judith Kelleher. *Brothels, Depravity, and Abandoned Women: Illegal Sex in Antebellum New Orleans*. Baton Rouge: Louisiana State University Press, 2009.

Szarkowski, John. *Bellocq*. New York: Random House, 1996.

————. *E.J. Bellocq: Storyville Portraits*. New York: Museum of Modern Art, 1970.

Tallant, Robert. *Voodoo in New Orleans*. N.p., 1946.

Additional Sources

"Ann Wilkinson Penrose Diary and Family Letters." 1861–65. MSS. 1169, Louisiana and Lower Mississippi Valley Collections, Louisiana State University Libraries.

Kelley, Laura D. "Yellow Fever." January 16, 2011. 64parishes.org.

"The Rise and Fall of John Law." *Historic New Orleans Collection Quarterly* 28, no. 4 (Fall 2011): 2–9.

Rothman, Adam. "The History of American Slavery: 'Nothing to Stay Here For.' How Enslaved People Helped to Put Slavery to Death in New Orleans." September 22, 2015. Slate.com.

"Succession of Mary A. Deubler, Docket No. 107603, 21667 and 22898." New Orleans Public Library.

Tom Anderson to Martin Behrman, 1908. Letter, Tulane University Special Collections, Howard-Tilton Memorial Library, Tulane University.

Newspapers

Colfax Chronicle, April 4, 1908.

Crowley Signal, November 19, 1910.

Louisiana Democrat, July 31, 1878.

Mascot, 1885.

————, August 3, 1889.

Montgomery Times, October 11, 1907.

New Orleans Item, May 27, 1881.

————, May 24, 1891.

————, September 1, 1893.

————, March 29, 1894.

————, July 12, 1903.

————, March 29, 1906.

————, February 19, 1914.

————, February 20, 1914.

————, March 1, 1914.

————, October 31, 1921.

New Orleans Item (published as the *Daily Item*), January 29, 1892.

————, December 24, 1901.

————, April 19, 1906.

————, 1919.

New Orleans States (published as the *Sunday States*), 1918.

New Orleans Weekly Democrat, July 7, 1877

Richland Beacon News, December 29, 1919.

Times Democrat, March 31, 1892.

————, March 17, 1914.

Times-Picayune, January 29, 1892.

————, April 20, 1903.

————, May 23, 1903.

————, January 14, 1905.

————, April 5, 1905.

————, December 2, 1905.

————, April 13, 1906.

————, April 20, 1906.

————, July 23, 1910.

————, April 29, 1911.

————, October 27, 1912.

————, February 21, 1914.

————, March 17, 1914.

————, June 25, 1978.

Vicksburg Evening Post, October 12, 1912.

Weekly Iberville South, February 16, 1878.

Websites

biblegateway.com

Bloodandmilk.com

Bustle.com

Corpse.org

Encyclopedia.com

BIBLIOGRAPHY

Infobarrel.com
kilmerhouse.com
Medicaldaily.com
old-new-orleans.com
people.loyno.edu
storyvilledistrictnola.com
themoonlitroad.com

ABOUT THE AUTHOR

Photo by Steven Crandle.

Marita Woywod Crandle, originally from Germany, moved to California with her parents at a young age. She became a marketing executive in California for several organizations, including Coldwell Banker, Home Savings of America and a product-driven company, Ashten. On a business trip to New Orleans, the city enchanted her, and she moved almost immediately to the French Quarter. She lives both in the French Quarter and by the lake with her husband, Steven Crandle, of New Orleans. Marita and her husband own Boutique du Vampyre, a vampire-themed gift shop, and manage Potions, their vampire-themed speakeasy, both in the French Quarter. Other books she has written include *New Orleans Vampires: History and Legend* and *Johnny White's Sports Bar: The Tiny Joint that Never Closed until It Did*, both for The History Press. She is currently writing a historical fiction vampire novel, *The Carter Brothers*, in which Josie Arlington is a featured character.

Visit us at
www.historypress.com